A Landscape of the Soul

One Poet's Journey Through Loss, Grief and Transformation

Grant Elgin Keller

One Beat Press
Los Angeles

One Beat Press
Los Angeles 2011

A Landscape of the Soul is published by One Beat Press.

ISBN: 978-0-9839883-1-1

To Aaron, for showing me joy in the heart of sorrow.

To my Muse, for opening my understanding.

The life given us, by nature is short; but the memory of a well-spent life is eternal ... The life of the dead is placed in the memory of the living.

Marcus Tullius Cicero

Table of Contents

Your pain is the breaking of the shell that encloses your understanding … It is the bitter potion by which the physician within you heals your sick self. Therefore, trust the physician, and drink his remedy in silence and tranquility. For his hand, though heavy and hard, is guided by the tender hand of the Unseen.

Kahlil Gibran

List of Poems

Prologue to the Journey

We will all, at times, know loss.

My Loss

My son Aaron was driving home from a movie when a young man in a convertible, fleeing from the police, struck Aaron's car at high speed. Aaron and his partner Jacob were crushed in an instant—at least I pray it was too quick for them to suffer. Jacob was like a second son to me, and I still miss both of them dreadfully. They were taken from me, but I like to believe that they are forever together now.

It happened on a hot August night in downtown Hollywood. Sunset Boulevard was filled that Friday evening with young people cruising up and down the Boulevard to see, and be seen. A generation earlier, I was part of that scene.

The air was electric with a hint of danger, pregnant with possibilities. Everyone in the crowd searching for people they knew or wanted to know, yelling and flirting, flashing their lures of attraction. Tattooed sleeves on muscled arms and thin white tank-tops. Low cut blouses and swaying hips in skintight jeans. Gang bangers and black lipped Goths, rappers and waifs, freaks and geeks, cheerleaders and transvestites, sometimes in the same body, rich kids and castaways, junkies and jocks, see me, want me, fear me, respect me, all swirling forward in a hip carnival atmosphere. Friday night on Sunset.

On those weekend nights, Sunset traffic is all but gridlocked by the mass of cars slowly cruising the streets. The local merchants complain that business suffers, so a multidivisional police task force was busy that night trying to control the cruisers. Sunset Boulevard and the surrounding streets were saturated with law enforcement officers from the Los Angeles Police Department, the County Sheriff's Department and the California Highway Patrol.

A Volkswagen convertible drove along Sunset in the sluggish stream of traffic. The car was filled with young men who were flirting with a group of laughing girls in a nearby car. During the trial, police officers admitted that the young man who was driving had not violated any traffic laws at that point. The driver did make a mistake when he tried to get closer to the girls by changing lanes in front of an all-black, unmarked car driven by a highway patrol lieutenant. This act seemed to upset the lieutenant who was in charge of the task force. His job that night was to watch for suspected cruisers and radio the license plate numbers of those cars to the officers ahead, who would safely pull them over and arrest, or ticket and release them.

Instead of following his orders, the lieutenant turned on his hidden emergency lights and started to chase the convertible. The easier solution would have been to radio ahead to the patrol cars already stationed near the intersection and have them drive forward a few feet to block all traffic. I suppose boredom, and the fact that the young men were all African-Americans wearing rapper style do-rags on their heads, may have influenced the lieutenant's decision—but that is just my guess.

Unfortunately, the driver of the convertible was a felon who didn't want to go back to prison. He tried to flee but the legal lanes were blocked, so he drove recklessly into oncoming traffic on one of the busiest streets in Hollywood, with the lieutenant in hot pursuit. Several witnesses, who observed the high speed chase from different vantage points along its entire length, agreed that the black car was always one car length behind the Volkswagen. The two cars sped to the nearest intersection and careened around the corner, scattering pedestrians who were in the crosswalk. The chase continued down a narrow residential street at speeds exceeding 90 miles per hour.

My son was driving his car along a cross street when the two cars drove through a stop sign at high speed. The convertible struck the passenger door of my son's car. The crime scene analysis of the skid marks in the intersection showed that the young man never applied his brakes, and apparently tried to drive through my son's car like he was acting out a part in a movie. Reality is far crueler. My son's car was spun into the path of an oncoming car. That horrified driver was unable to react in time and his car plowed into the driver's door of my son's car. Our two boys were crushed to death by the twin impacts.

A motorist, who was driving a few cars behind my son, testified that there was no warning, no siren, just a flash of light and an explosion of glass when the cars collided. I saw the wreck of my son's car; the driver and passenger doors were touching inside. Oddly, none of the young men in the Volkswagen were injured.

Antwan, the young man who killed Aaron and Jacob, would later be convicted of two counts of murder for his reckless disregard of the public safety that night. This is the terrible price innocents pay in all too many high speed chases. The lieutenant who initiated the chase testified under oath that he had violated no traffic laws. The law gave him complete immunity.

Death did not stop there. The moment Jacob's father heard of his son's death, he suffered a heart attack and died a few days later. You can die of a broken heart. I too felt that my life ended that night with Aaron's, but I eventually learned to accept my loss and found the strength to continue.

My Grief

Initially, I felt a tremendous shock that gave way to anger and denial. After the funeral my denial deepened as my anger faded. I withdrew from personal contact to sit in sorrow and look inward for answers.

After some time searching inside for understanding, I directed my attention outward at the great injustice of his death. Anger then reasserted itself ripping away the deadening wool of denial.

My anger was white hot, mixed with hatred for my son's killer. A fierce desire for vengeance twisted in my guts. I was flooded with the twin poisons of guilt and shame; guilt for my inability to prevent his death, and shame for my hatred. I tried to bargain with God to bring back the son I should have protected and take me instead. When I finally saw the futility of all my raging emotions, I fell into a deep depression.

All through my changing emotional states I repeatedly experienced soul searing outward spasms of grief followed by periods of deep sorrow where I searched inward for answers and an understanding of my loss. Tearful wailing agony was followed by quiet healing.

Breaking through all this storm and thunder were quiet moments of peace, humor, and wry observation. All these unlikely contrasting emotions were necessary for my survival and were a sign of my essential resilience, a resilience we all share. Every bout with grief led me to growing degrees of acceptance and (eventually) resolution and joy. Yes, there is joy, even in the heart of sorrow.

My Poetry

This book is unlike other books of poetry. My poems are the record of my journey through the landscape of my soul—my progress through the process of grief. The death of my son destroyed my faith in myself and everything I believed to be real, and good, in the world. I lost trust in myself and the very nature of the universe. My inner landscape was ravaged and laid bare, transformed into a raw and alien wasteland.

As I walked my painful path through grieving, I rebuilt my faith and trust—recreating that landscape anew. I learned how to gain wisdom from pain and sorrow and use it to rekindle happiness and joy in my changed life. I discovered how to project my will on the universe and create pattern from chaos. This is the essential role we all play when we live our true, authentic lives. We all are creators, and these poems show how I discovered this truth.

I am an unlikely poet. I don't even own a beret. Other than memorizing some Shakespeare and Kipling in high school, I didn't pay much attention to poetry. Oh, I liked when I read it, but it all seemed kind of, well—fussy. I never saw myself as a poet; however, I did have great respect for my son's ability to express his inner emotions in this medium. I just never saw myself doing it. When I rescued Aaron's poetry from the massive pile of letters, bills and school papers he left behind, I read them with fresh eyes. This must have sparked something inside me, unlocked a door I had shut before he was born. Aaron is now my silent writing companion.

When confronted with grief, I tried to capture my extreme emotional states in the fewest possible words. I needed to record them, understand what they meant to me, and share them. I was surprised to find I was writing poetry—the distilled spirits of my emotions. I wrote them, simply because I had to.

I am not a psychiatrist, therapist, or grief counselor. I am just a guy who has been tested hard by loss. I experienced the deepest form of grief, that of a parent for a child.

I cannot write a prescription for your pain, but I can tell you how grief shook my world for a time. I can explain how I learned to hack the mechanisms of grief to gain a measure of control over the extreme emotions I was experiencing, and how I used those mechanisms to completely transform myself into a better and happier person.

My poems describe grief, the healing process of recovery from loss. The goal of grief is to gain an acceptance of our loss, what our loss means to us, and how loss changed our life. The essential nature of grief is transformational. Loss changes us, and we adapt to loss in our grieving. My poems show how I progressed through the grief process to acceptance, and how I hacked grief to emerge a better and freer person. One more suited to achieve a new, and higher, level of consciousness and happiness.

I responded to grief by experiencing several powerful recurring emotional states. One of the states was a deep sorrow that caused me to look inward to understand my loss. I found it was possible to use this inward search to examine those parts of myself that had always held me back, and understand how they prevented me from living a full and happy life.

When I started this book, I planned on sharing my poems about the experiences of my loss, and how I came to terms with that loss. While I was writing, I found that I had to do more. I also needed to explain how I learned to use grief to transform myself. When we lose someone who is important to us, we use the mechanism of grief to figure out what happened. First, this powerful internal process helped me to understand how my son could been taken from me and what his loss meant to me. Then, I learned how deeply his loss changed me. Finally, I learned how I could go forward in my changed life without him. Each of these hard lessons helped me come to another layer of acceptance.

After I collected all my poems about grief, I knew that wasn't the entire story. Even in the darkest episodes of grief I would sometimes find myself thinking about joy. Occasionally, grief can even bring us a moment of humor to help lighten our load. I found the need to also write poems about happiness, growth and love. These poems explored other parts of my internal landscape, and without them this journey would not be complete. Even in the heart of sorrow we will find joy, because we are human. Nothing can keep us down for long. We are wonderfully resilient and adaptable beings.

Who is This Book for?

Death, growing apart, moving away, all result in the loss of important people from our lives. Some of us will feel the loss of love in a relationship, or in a divorce. That kind of loss will be painful, and we will grieve. Some of us will lose our health and that too brings on grief. For some, the loss of health leads to our final act of grief. Every form of loss requires some measure of grieving to deal with the pain, sorrow, and changes in our lives. Eventually we learn to accept our loss and continue on in a changed reality. Grief heals.

We all approach grief in different ways, but there are some similarities in the experience. One thing is certain, we will all experience loss and grief at some time in our lives, as have our ancestors. Grief is a universal condition of life and death, of having and losing. When we learn from grief, we will all be given the opportunity to share the wealth of our experiences with others. Grief shared is grief lessened.

I believe we can help each other with our grieving by sharing our experiences. In spite of our differences, aren't we all the same at some level? Don't we all connect? Aren't we all beings of energy, passion, love and joy?

In *The Power of Myth*, Joseph Campbell discussed Schopenhauer's belief that you and I are one, two aspects of one life, and our apparent separateness is merely an artifact of the limited way we perceive time and space. We are in control of our reality filters and can change our perceptions.

I find it comforting to live with a clear awareness of our connections. I believe, with Schopenhauer, that this is one of the fundamental truths of our lives. We are all one. I wrote this book as a celebration of our connections, for those tough moments when we need to understand and help each other. This book is for all of us when we know grief.

My Path

As we walk through my poems, please understand that my actual path was not as linear as the 'stages' suggest. The stages are only a convenient way of organizing my poems to reveal the inner emotional states I experienced during my journey. Your path will be unique to your loss, but you will experience some, or all, of the same emotional states I did. This organization of poems makes it easier for you to find the right poem to read according to how you are feeling.

Sometimes, I wandered lost on my path. Other times I charged boldly ahead looking for a fight. I would double back and revisit a place I needed to know better, a place that needed more attention. I would often go into my dark side to revisit old hidden wounds and wrestle with my dragons. This inner work of confronting and accepting my shadow self was vital to making me a complete person armed with the power and strength of my true self.

There were times I would tarry with laughter and joy in a peaceful spot and rest, drink of the wellspring of my power to refresh my resolve, and gather strength for my next assault. I wandered at times, or spiraled in on a difficult objective, but always I moved forward in my acceptance no matter where I went on my path.

By reading this book, you are joining me in a journey through the landscape of a soul that loss changed. I will show you some of the features of the new world I found and a bit about how I shaped that landscape to form a better world for me.

It is my sincere hope that these observations will help you with your grieving so you emerge, not only whole in your acceptance, but a better and more complete person. I hope they help you discover the empathy that will let you show compassionate care for someone else who is suffering. For now, please walk the path with me a while as we explore this strange landscape of a soul.

We live under the assumption that if we are just, we will not suffer. But to have life is to know death. To love is ultimately to lose what we have had the privilege of loving.

Elisabeth Kübler-Ross

Chapter One

I Start my Journey

loss — the thief of faith
blinds us to the balm of hope
time is compassion

3 AM — AND THE DOORBELL SPLITS THE NIGHT.
A surge of adrenaline rockets me from my bed and down the stairs. Lisa, my wife, following close behind. Heart pounding in my chest, I throw open the front door to find my sister-in-law soaking wet from the sprinklers in my yard. What the hell? "Come in. I — I'm sorry. The timer." I stammer.

She and my brother-in-law brush soundlessly past me into the room, they stop and turn to me. "There's been an accident," she says with a stricken face, "Mijo is dead." Lisa wails anguish from her soul and falls into her sister's arms. The room crashes in upon me. My son is dead.

The air around me thickens and turns to amber, fixing me in my place. I want to force the words back into her mouth. To push back time, make it change back. I'm desperate to make this NOT HAPPEN, but I'm powerless to stop the flow of words—the torrent that threatens to drown me in sorrow.

I have a thousand questions that beg answers, and I have no mouth to speak. Shock hammers me and I wonder at water pooling on the floor. Where did it come from? Why is my face wet? Who are these screaming people?

Shock was my first memory of grief. Shock at the suddenness of loss. Shock at the unexpectedness of death at an early age. Shock at the flash of realization: my life was forever changed.

The Moment

I attempted to capture the moment I learned of my son's death in this poem. My faith in reality was broken, because I could not understand how he died so casually, so easily. Reality could not work the way I believed it did if this foul deed was true. Therefore, I reasoned in my pain, reality must be denied and I must abandon my trust in the essentially benevolent nature of God and everything good in the universe. It took a long time in my grieving to restore my faith and my trust; that restoration was part of my hard won acceptance.

Without trust I found I could not have a meaningful relationship with another person. One of the causalities of my loss of trust was my marriage. Lisa and I underwent couples therapy and eventually decided that divorce was the only way we could retain the long, and valued, friendship we shared since we were teenagers. Lisa is still a very important person in my life. I will always respect and love her.

The Moment

Shock slams into me driving air from my lungs

Words that cannot be—float motionless before me
shaping a terrible, crushing reality

that must be denied

The air changes, grows thick and yellow
this moment fixed forever in amber
the eternal moment my reality crashed

How can I force back the words
and halt the spill of pain?
My son cannot be dead

If just one link
in this terrible chain
of events could be unbound

perhaps my son would not be gone
perhaps my life would be unchanged
perhaps this pain would not bloom forth

perhaps—
but it cannot be
This terrible truth exists

I believed in a universe causal, not casual
cause and effect my root
Twin pillars of steel anchored firm in reason

but reason has somehow fled
No logic—only happenstance

That chance could steal so much from me defies conception
overwhelms comprehension
undermines the core of my existence

and strips away my faith, shattering encrusted dogma

I struggle to reweave the tangled strings of chaos

convinced by consistencies
that every event must have a cause

Belief in causality blinding me to reality's true nature

The universe remains chaotic
impervious to my efforts at control
Death comes for us all at a flick of fate

Tao just happens
Order is delusion
the universe *is* casual after all

Cherished perceptions shaped by old beliefs
prove to be merely patterns in the clouds
begat of chaos's butterflies

All attempts to bend back time's flow failed
I wandered lost without a guide

My beliefs broken, bereft of comfortable illusion

a lapsed pagan

Stripped bare by fate in a tattered world
afraid and unable to go it alone
I rise naked, humble before my creator

Finally, I know Job

Sometimes our souls are pummeled and stretched
reshaped by acceptance of flowing realities
made ready to embrace change with grace

and learn anew that faith sustains when reality falls short

God endures
love endures, and I will endure
struggling with faith to draw meaning from existence

Meltdown

I was actually in the midst of a grief spasm, or 'meltdown', when I wrote my first poem about the recurring episodes of grieving. I found I could bring an element of grief out of my body and examine it more closely. It was like holding part of my pain in my hands.

I had been suffering these episodes for two months before I thought to record my experiences. The meltdown happened when my former wife, Lisa, and I were driving home.

An old Johnny Mathis song came on the radio, and the words, "Why do the birds go on singing? … Don't they know it's the end of the world." were the trigger.

Lisa went into a meltdown, and I was not far behind. Back then it didn't take much to put me in the state of extreme grieving. I have not had a hard meltdown for some time now, but I at times I feel the echoes. I was suddenly aware of all the little triggers that so easily cause us to fall into grief.

I saw the endless cycle of grief episodes, and wanted to capture the idea that the cycling is normal and should not be feared. I had a sudden, uncontrollable urge to capture the emotions boiling inside of me. I went into one of the grief episodes and wrote from there. I described the landscape of that terrible new reality.

I warn you that *Meltdown* is filled with raw pain, but it serves as an introduction to the extreme emotions that overwhelm us in grief. If you have ever grieved for a loss, you will recognize this strange new landscape. The intensity of the features change according to the intensity of the loss, but the contours of the hills and valleys you encounter there will be familiar.

By tasting a bit of a meltdown in this way, you will have an easier time with the start of the healing process of grief. *Meltdown* serves as an inoculation against the massive assault of the early episodes of grief on your mind and body. There is also an element of endurance in this poem that I think is essential to understand. We suffer, we heal, and then we wait in the knowledge that more suffering will come. The meltdowns come when they need to come on a schedule all their own. The grieving process should never be rushed. We walk our path at our own pace. It's important to remember that you will never be given more pain than you can handle at any moment.

Meltdown

A song, a scent, a photograph
a silly commercial once shared with my lost one
triggers a stuttering heave in my chest

and I slide down the darkling path of grief

My throat squeezes shut to smother a sob
My eyes fill with tears pushed out
by swelling pressure in my head

until hot oil burns down my face
All that exists is the crashing implosion of my world
squeezing my soul into the black hole of my heart

Everything falls inward

My knees fail and cannot resist the titanic weight of my loss

Sounds stop. Smells stop
Vision hides behind a shimmer of tears

My heart tries to force its way up past a crushing throat
Silent coughs jerk my chest in sync
with the squeezing rhythm in my heart

My head nods with the spasms of grief
and I rock back and forth in a cocoon of dark
wrapped around the ache where my heart should be

I have always been here and will never leave
Fixed in this timeless throb of loss
Slowly the outside intrudes

Self-consciousness steals the freedom of abandon

Sounds return. Smells bloom
Vision clears to readmit
the constricts of shared reality

I rub oily tears from my face
gasp in the world in shuddering gulps

and wait for the next trigger

~

Love Invoked

In contrast to *Meltdown*, several months later I wrote *Love Invoked* which captured me in a stronger, and more resilient, state of mind. It was less than a year after my loss, and I was faced with yet another death.

My mother-in-law died, and I was asked to write something for her funeral service.

I had suffered so many losses already—my mother, my father, my son—and now another. I wondered then if my losses would ever end.

I had started to come to terms with the sharpest part of grief, but I was still numb. Sorrow again turned my attention inward, and I saw that all I could really hold on to were fluttering fragments of the memories I shared with my lost ones. I drew comfort from the love invoked by those memories, no matter how painful it still was to hold them.

Love Invoked

Sitting in solemn solitude
I view a life fragmented

No tears: just now
Grief dulled by repetition
the agony of loss at bay for a time

I dwell

Struck still in the moment, locked in reverie
Bewildered, benumbed, entranced
unable to connect the shattered bits

so precious, so fragile

Small snatches of memory, scattered about me
flit through my consciousness, compelling attention
teasing me from the now

Gifting me with cherished moments
time shards once shared, rich in joy and pain
gingerly held in bleeding fingers

I behold the sweet entanglements of life
glittering threads of existence, traced through time and space
twisted in glowing knots embedded in the dark

My soul unfolds to them, filling the void of loss

drawing life from memory
meaning from tragedy
empathy from pain

I learn to walk anew
to see again with newborn eyes
the path to my salvation

Slowly healing in the balm of time
I gain solace from love invoked

~

Chapter Two

Dark Night of the Soul

2

embrace tonight's pain
tomorrow pledges solace
hope reborn each dawn

The cyclic episodes of grief continued to test me at every step of my journey, and I was gaining a little experience with sorrow's inward search for understanding. It was then, a few months after the death of my son, that I encountered my most profound trial. I lived through my 'dark night of the soul' in the Carmel Highlands of California. I was having a difficult time sorting out my tangled emotions and Los Angeles held too many memories for me.

Everywhere I looked I found things that triggered my grief episodes. I decided to spend some time in a completely different environment and a friend suggested I try a peaceful spot she knew about in Carmel. It was also the weekend of my wedding anniversary, and Lisa and I just wanted to be in a quiet place. We didn't feel much like celebrating.

The snug little Inn was perched on a cliff with a magnificent view of the ocean. Our room opened onto a large wooden balcony facing the water. Other than the cries of a few lonely seagulls, the only sound came from the waves relentlessly hurling themselves against the rocks below. It was peaceful during the day and I started to let down my guard.

I went out on the balcony to watch the waves come in, while Lisa slept restlessly inside. I was just starting to relax when the sun fled, leaving behind a black sky filled with stars. There were so *many* stars. Millions of eyes staring into my soul. Cold air slid icy fingers through my clothes, and I started shivering. I lay down on the wood recliner, wrapped a blanket around me and listened to the waves.

I woke up with a start in the early hours of the morning and went to the railing. I stood terrified and alone on that balcony, looking upward into the night, while the waves were crashing below me in the dark. There are few lights on the coast in that area, so nothing diminished the full, soul-crushing impact of the stars when I looked outward into the void.

I was torn by my loss and felt very small and permeable. The terror of that night came upon me with full force, as I struggled with the necessity to choose life or death. Do I continue in my struggle, or do I give in to my fears and step off the balcony?

I had survived onslaught after onslaught and wasn't sure I wanted to continue the fight. I felt beaten, bloody and bone weary. I didn't know where I could find the strength to contain any longer the massive pain of loss that seemed to fill and strain every fiber of my being. I felt that I was about to be rent open by the stresses within.

The rocks below pulled at me, promising a swift end to my endless pain. All seemed lost and beyond my grasp. I wept and let go the last of my restraints, doubts and fears.

I could no longer live with who I had become, this creature of pain, so I had to push forward. In my moment of surrender I took my final step to defy my pain. I felt the darkness shiver through me, and then an enormous weight was pulled from me.

RELEASE

I sat drained and humbled, suspended between twin oceans of darkness, and encapsulated the experience in the poem *release*. That act of containment placed bounds on the emotions of despair and abandonment that threatened to pull me to my destruction.

release

3 AM

Standing at cliff's edge
under a riot of stars

Soft whispers from a restless sea, lost within the void of night
suck marrow from my soul

I lean forward into the dark, fixed by the abyss
primal fear sleeting through quaking flesh

expecting teeth, a claw from behind, a stab of fright

Alone with loss
afraid to breathe, afraid to look

With a start, a racking sob shakes me

I loosen my grip on fear, and pain flows out with my tears

Shuddering into the depths, burning as it flees
Leaving me open, empty

ready to be filled

aching for the touch of god

~

Capture Rapture

I sat empty in exhaustion for a time in the dark. I was reluctant to move until I heard birdsong greeting the return of the light. I stood to face the ocean and stretched out my arms and legs as far as they could go, feeling new strength flowing into me. I drank in the dawn and filled emptiness with resolve and strength. I could feel my new found power snapping inside me. I felt heroic beyond measure.

I was alive and glad of it. The burdens that were unbearable in the dark, were now easy to carry. The obstacles that were insurmountable could now be overcome. Weariness vanished, replaced with strength welling up from an inexhaustible source within. I shed my old self that night and transformed into a soul warrior, suited for battle. I knew that I only had to envision what I wanted and reality would conform to my will. I still had a long, hard struggle waiting for me, but I was now ready for whatever lay ahead on my path to acceptance.

When I took that one step forward into the darkness, instead of a leap of despair, I chose a leap of faith. My first act of faith was to trust myself. I chose to live beyond the night, and with the dawn came my answer. I wrote Capture Rapture. This clear exclamation of my love for life is halfway between a prayer, and an ancient spell-casting.

I am struck with the difference between these two poems written only a few hours apart. That sharp contrast is a reminder that when circumstance challenged me, and my future looked hopelessly bleak, a few hours of patience rewarded me with fresh insights and a renewal of my lost hope. If you find yourself on that balcony—push beyond your pain and wait until the light returns to you before making your decision. It's hard to see clearly when surrounded by darkness.

Capture Rapture has become my favorite poem, and was my steady guide through my transformation. It has become my manifesto. It speaks of the process of pulling desire from within to impose pattern on the world without—creating our reality from chaos. A declaration of power that taught me the art of seeing and applying the magic that surrounds us at every moment. It reminds me to look clearly, understand what I see, and create my life as art.

Capture Rapture

See the ocean in a drop
the loaf in a grain, the wine in a grape

Stand open to awe
shudder and quake

Let your power shiver through
to unlock joy, to drive out pain
to heal the ragged wounds of loss, and awaken hope

Capture Rapture

Use it to mine the clay of creation
Imagine your deep, hidden desires, and craft them

Breathe deep and savor the quickening movement of change
Grab tight the torrent, twist and bend it to your will

guide it outward

Fill your world with visions made real

~

My grief driven trips through sorrow and introspection gave me a better understanding of my loss, but also revealed the nature of my inner self. Grief stripped away the clouds hiding my buried wounds, fears and weaknesses and let me see how these false constraints held me back from fully living my life. I saw how I let the bad experiences and misunderstandings of my past limit the healthy growth of my body, mind and spirit. My stubborn resistance to change prevented me from accepting the internal advances that set the stage for my emergence from that dark night. I had reclaimed my sword, but I would not see it clutched in my hand.

It was only later that I learned about the work of the 16th century poet and mystic, Juan de la Cruz. He was undergoing a crisis of faith and wrote a poem about the loneliness and desolation he experienced when he felt God had abandoned him. He too embraced the pain of his separation during his dark night. When I learned that he was a priest of the Brothers of Our Lady of Mount Carmel, I realized that the Carmel Highlands were very appropriate for my own crisis of faith.

We sometimes find ourselves in places where we are meant to be, even if we don't understand why we are drawn there. Are these the nudging actions of a benevolent Creator, or cold acts of irony?

All I know for sure was that I belonged in that healing place, and I found solace in the poems I wrote for wounds that were still fresh and raw. It was there I found my purpose, my need to create. It was there I found my true self, armed with the strength to follow my path to acceptance and my new life.

Fools Flight

In spite of the powerful advances I made during my trial that night, it took me another eight months before I could go beyond my faith in myself, and restore my trust in the benevolent nature of my Creator and the universe.

Fool's Flight is the final poem that resulted from my experiences during that dark night. The poem describes how it feels to dare fate and step out into the unknown, not caring what comes next.

I tried to capture the rush of feelings that comes to me when I start something new. I was at a place of new beginnings in my life, and I felt like a little child again.

This time when I stood at the edge of a cliff, I felt excitement instead of fear. I was ready to fly and soar over that landscape in front of me. I knew that it wasn't rational to leap off the cliff, but I discovered that there are times when actions are needed that are not based on rational thought.

My old programming was leading me to logical conclusions that were no longer valid in my changed reality. I had to trust my intuition and take that thrilling leap into my future, trusting that I would learn to fly before I crashed. It was hard to trust anything after my loss, but I knew intuitively that it was time to extend my trust again. For a long time, the arms that lifted me up in the poem were my own, but I knew I was now ready to open myself to others.

Fool's Flight

I am the fool at the precipice
struck dumb at the sight of dawn's creation
Standing poised to fall, heeding not the planet's pull

Freshening winds howl up the cliff to buffet me
tearing, pulling, teasing my hair
snatching out both words and thought

A blossoming beauty of light
draws me forward

I move, ignorant of danger

Forcing myself to breath
I suck in erotic, magnificent perfume

I fill a reeling head with sweet intoxications
and grow giddy with exploding visions
Bursting with anticipation I step forward

swaying in the music of the wind
With rising conviction
I gather myself, muscles quaking in expectation

I draw close the scattered elements of my soul
drink deeply of the day
and abandon gravity's cold and leaden chains

I leap — trusting in flight

Plummeting, trailing wisps of cloud
fear sleeting through, thrumming me like crystal
heart thrilling in an ecstasy of fear

I spin into the mist

Pulled forward, upward by love
grasping tight the outstretched hands
I soar on quivering wings over landscapes fresh and wondrous

Singing in joy I wrap myself in you

~

Chapter Three

Poems of Denial

3

truth that cannot be
rends my soul with cruel intent
spare me this moment

When I first heard the news that my son was dead I went into denial. I was not denying his actual death. It was just that the entirety of the experience was simply too much for me to cope with at one time. I didn't want it to be true, so it couldn't be true. My psyche protected me from the full impact of loss by giving me a little time to come to terms with a changed reality that I was not yet ready to accept. I hoped that it was all a mistake, and I was in some kind of horrible dream. I felt he was just out there, somewhere, and would soon return. I would walk into a room, certain he was waiting for me, only to be stunned when he was nowhere to be seen.

I had a dream that illustrated my denial. In my dream, I woke in the darkness to hear muted sobbing. I followed the sounds down the hall to my son's room, and saw him curled up on his bed with his back to me. I felt joy and relief that his death was all a mistake. Here he was, safe in his bed. I walked quietly to him and reached out to touch his shoulder, so I could comfort him. His head started to turn, and when I touched him he vanished. Grief slammed me to the carpet, and I woke to find myself sobbing in his room, alone. Denial gave me one short moment of relief and joy before sorrow reclaimed me. I think that was my first, hard moment of acceptance. Denial helps us to survive.

Fragile Edge of Grief

Part of my denial was a feeling of separation, or distance, from the rest of the world. I needed some time to be alone with my grief. I found I was compelled to look into myself and search for clues that would help me understand what was happening to me.

I later learned that this inward directed search for meaning is part of how sorrow works on us, and it was a vital step forward in my healing. I sat, sometimes for hours, in a seemingly befuddled state.

Denial wrapped me in a mental cocoon that gave me a temporary respite from the sharpness of my pain—so I could rest. *Fragile Edge of Grief* captures some of the feelings of that detached state I dwelled in. I skirted the edge of my grief in a fragile balance I could not continue for long.

Eventually, my loss intruded and wiped away all the deadening wool from my mind. I fell once more into the hot spasms of pain. Grief was teaching me how to bite off a bit of my pain and consume it, one bite at a time, over and over again.

Fragile Edge of Grief

Confused, detached, estranged from the real
I sit. Not so much somber, but distracted
The sharp pain of loss somewhat dulled for the moment

Unable to focus clearly on my work
math skills muddled, simple mistakes creep in

Unsure how to proceed, but unwilling to go back

Not to the white hot, all consuming burn of heartache
the helpless, hopeless abandonment of self
the choking need to vomit out pain and sorrow

I sit instead, unmoving for hours

Contemplating my un-connectedness
Staring at an unfinished sentence, puzzled by coffee gone cold
wondering idly where time had gone

I start a note to aid my forgetfulness, and forget what to write
I halt in mid task, confused, frustrated, uncertain
Action now out of reach, goal fled from consciousness

I breathe deep
sigh into my hands
and rock in overload with covered eyes

Driven to this place by an unendurable strain of truth
an inescapable comprehension of a harsh reality
A world empty of my beloved

Afraid to make decisions
but forced to choose
by a relentless world

Slowed by lethargy, left behind
unable to reenter the swift flow of time
Vulnerable. Breakable

Skirting the fragile edge of grief

Blindsided

Sometimes the meltdowns of grief surprised me, taking me over when I least expected it. *Blindsided* reveals the cyclic nature of grieving as a process of destruction and recreation. My time worn beliefs were challenged by the impact of loss on my life.

I thought I understood how reality worked, only to find what I once believed to be true and fair did not allow for this loss. This was part of my denial. My beliefs, hopes, and expectations were destroyed and had to be recreated.

As I passed through many onslaughts of grieving, my meltdowns, I eventually saw that the full impact of loss was simply too much for me to endure at one time.

Mercifully, I only suffered a bit of grief during each episode and then spent some time healing. This extended the duration of my grieving process, so I was only given as much pain as I could handle at any moment. My unique needs were driving the schedule of my grief; we should never try to rush our grieving. As my understanding continued to expand, I came to a growing acceptance of my loss.

Elisabeth Kübler-Ross mentioned this partitioning of grief into manageable portions in her book, *On Grief and Grieving*. She explained that denial is our Psyche's protective mechanism for, "letting in only as much as we can handle." She goes on to state, "Letting in all the feelings associated with loss at once would be overwhelming emotionally. We can't believe what has happened because we actually *can't* believe what has happened. To fully believe at this stage would be too much."

It was my experience that this protective mechanism continued throughout the entire grieving process. I kept getting doses of grief, followed by periods of healing.

Blindsided

I thought at last I understood grief
slowly gaining control these last few weeks
finding space to breathe

I still had meltdowns
but not so intense
not so painful as before

I knew grief is a long process
the work of years
but felt the worst had past

I am the Fool

I blinked and the world crashed again
exquisite pain driving me to depths unknown
unsuspected, crushing in gravity

Head pounding, gasping for air, caught unprepared
Blindsided in an instant with terrible choking
quiet sobbing, a wracking pain of loss

A bubble of grief grew in my chest
ready to burst
aching to break free

thrummed in my heart
expanding inexorably up my throat
pressing under my chin

forcing me to the cliff
to stand again before the void
and step over

It was different this time
fewer tears than before
but the ache was deep, so very deep

Shattering my control
shaking my soul
My body reeling, drunk with stress poisons

unsteady, unbalanced
unable to control my hands or my actions
I didn't know about the levels

The Dantesque layer cake of destruction and recreation
Destruction of once cherished beliefs
hopes, expectations, dreams

Recreation of self, soul
understanding of this ephemera
existence

I didn't know that grief would wait
give you time to heal from the last trial
Let you gather strength

prepare yourself in ignorance for another onslaught
That when it felt you were ready
would reveal a whole new level of grief

This is not cruelty, not malice
not the whim of an capricious capering god
Grief is our ancient survival programming

teaching how to deal with loss
without growing callus on our essential humanity
to retain our compassion, empathy

Grief teaches resilience, helps us adapt
helps us to grasp each moment
Taking nothing for granted

to understand the ephemeral nature of being
to realize all plans are based in belief of the status quo
to hold nothing back, to savor life and love now

Tomorrow is illusion

Grief uses pain, the swift teacher
Grief is the gauntlet we run to gain acceptance of loss
deepening our changed relationship with our lost one

and with our God

Eventually, it brings us to peace within our self
in that solitary place wherein we dwell
We must ignore fear, embrace grief and let pain teach

Grief will knock you off your complacent plateau
cast you again into transforming fire
Hammer, forge and temper you

leaving you reformed anew of stronger metal
better able to withstand the stress of a changed reality
prepared for new levels of grief

~

Known in the Bones

I was rereading *Blindsided* and reflecting on the idea that grief is our ancient survival programming. I recalled a message I received a few days earlier from a friend of mine who wrote to console me, saying he could relate to the pain I was in. He told me that he and his wife had just lost their twin boys at birth. As a father of twins, their loss touched me deeply.

In my attempt to ease their pain, I wrote back, "I am starting to understand that the joys we cherish, and sorrows we survive, shape the landscape of our souls." He said this little line was helpful to both his wife and himself.

I wrote that line on my computer, and to my astonishment my next poem, *Known in the Bones,* came flowing out. The thought that grief is our ancient survival programming gave structure to this new poem. Grief teaches us how to deal with loss without growing callus on our essential humanity. This way we retain our capability to recognize, and understand, the pain of fellow sufferers. This is our very essential capacity for empathy.

Empathy is based on the Greek word for feeling or suffering. Empathy is, quite literally, the feeling of another's pain and the understanding of their suffering. Grief is filled with sorrow and brings us an intimate understanding of pain. Empathy opens us to this pain. To know our own pain, is to know the pain of another. When we truly experience pain we would not wish it on anyone.

Empathetic understanding leads us to compassion. Compassion is from the Latin word meaning 'to suffer with'. Compassion is suffering with another and, as a result, wanting to ease that suffering with compassionate care. When we suffer with someone we help to lessen their sorrow. Compassionate sharing of another's suffering forms a connection deep intimacy and trust. That intimacy can bring us a great joy. In this manner, we can find joy in the heart of sorrow.

Known in the Bones

I am starting to understand that the joys we cherish
and sorrows we survive
shape the landscape of our souls

I am slowly coming to learn
In grief that landscape is laid bare
starkly lit by the raw light of a shifted reality

Our comfortable, well-worn path is gone
The quiet glades, trails we loved to walk
vanished

Our landmarks, nowhere to be found

our direction, confused
our thinking, muddled
all familiar, twisted

All that remains is a terrible new path to walk
A path that flows in undulating waves
across an alien plane

A path known in the bones of our ancestors

wisdom of the grave

One thousand generations and more
have walked this path
and gone beyond, but

for each of us, for each new loss
the path is fresh and leads to places we cannot know
until we reach them

The path will not be denied, however we try to trick ourselves

Denial snares us. We don't want it to be true
We pretend that they are still out there
and are just distracted by life

They are just busy now
they will call any day now
they will walk grinning through the door now

shouting that is was all a mistake

An obscene error
It did not happen to them
It was someone else's loss

But they won't. They can't
The cruel new reality that is
will not let that be

So—we face the real

and walk the path
Letting it take us where it must

To deny is to face falsehood
to lose our-selves following false trails
to lose our-souls chasing false hopes

The path teaches us to accept
We learn to live in a world
in which they are not

We learn to go on, to survive the loss
To deny the power of death by creating new features
in the landscape of our souls

~

Chapter Four

Poems of Anger and Vengeance

vengeance burns my blood
anger chills my heart to ice
pain must answer pain

EVENTUALLY, DENIAL LOOSENED ITS DEADENING grip on me, and I started to feel my anger at the injustice of my loss. I didn't ask for this to happen to me. I couldn't understand how it could have happened. Now I was forced to deal with it. My world had been shattered, and I had to put the jagged pieces back together with blood stained fingers. It HURT and I was ANGRY.

I felt guilt and shame over the loss. Even though it wasn't rational, I was angry with myself for not preventing the loss. I was my son's protector, and I couldn't protect him. I thought if I had acted differently he wouldn't have died.

I was deeply ashamed when, in my raging anger, I even blamed him for not being more careful and for leaving me, even though I knew he did nothing wrong. Anger respects no bounds or reason, often giving us fertile ground for growing guilt and shame. I know now that these poisonous feelings are typical responses to grief, and also that they aren't true. I can't chastise myself forever for my momentary lapses of sense. I must accept I'm only human. I can't take responsibility for everything that happens in this world. I just don't have that kind of power.

I then directed my anger outward to seek its proper target. The man who took my son from me. My anger at my son's killer taught me that it's important to give voice to anger and not suppress it. I discovered that strong feelings of anger are normal, and very human, expressions of love and loss. Trying to forgive too soon does not allow us to fully realize the impact of the wrong done to us. I needed to feel the anger, and understand it, before I could move to forgiveness. I had to know what my loss cost me, so I would know what I was forgiving.

Anger is useful for a while but, like vengeance, hatred, guilt and shame, anger serves no long term purpose. These feelings are only spurs to help us move through the grief processing. They are goads to understanding. I experienced all of these deep emotions during my grieving, and they led me to my eventual understanding and acceptance of loss. I had to remember they were only transitory emotions, and I must discard them after they served their purpose.

Probably, the most profound grief is that of a parent for the death of a child. Our children are supposed to outlive us. We are not supposed to bury them. If the death is violent, and unexpected, the grief can be even deeper. That is the grief that changed me forever.

I hated the man who killed my son, and I lusted for vengeance. When I first sat in the courtroom to witness his trial, I carefully measured in my mind the distance from me to that young man. I looked at the placement of the armed guards in the court. I can still taste the bitterness of disappointment when I realized they would stop me before I could get to him. I wanted nothing more than to take his life, as he had taken my son's.

Night Flight

During the trial, I started having dreams that resembled mad slasher movies, with me cast in the role of the slasher. *Night Flight,* captures the feelings of hatred, blood lust, and frustration I felt in those days. I knew a fierce need to hurt the man who snuffed out the bright life of my son, and brought me to this place of darkness. I stopped having these dreams only when I realized I wasn't living out a retribution movie, rather I was enduring a hard and cold reality. I just could not do those things to another person, no matter how evil he seemed to me. I would have to settle for justice instead of blood.

Night Flight

I chase my prey through dreams
trapping him in a killing place

Grasping him about the neck
squeezing with my entire being

I pour the irresistible force of need through shaking hands

Driven by necessity to end this life
to erase the wrong, avenge the loss

restore reality once more to its proper course

The stubble on his neck pricks my hands
as they close tighter

The cartilage of his windpipe crackles
and starts to give way

slowly succumbing to the strength of my attack

Rough cabin floorboards press their image
into the skin of my knees

Rustic walls enclose the unfolding drama
absorbing each moment

capturing each sound, observing but not judging

The prey starts to smile
ignoring my punishment

The harder I clutch in desperation
the more I squeeze—the more it grins

smug in the knowledge of my impotence

I find I'm only grasping air
grappling shadows

I shake with thwarted rage
and sob with abandon

Stricken again by sudden loss—I despair

My prey has fled again, gone once more beyond my reach
leaving me alone, distraught

wrapped tight once more in sorrow's solitude

~

Anger Burning Cold

My desire for vengeance passed but not my deep, almost blinding, anger. That is when I wrote *Anger Burning Cold.* I felt I had mastered and released my need for vengeance, but it's easier to give up vengeance than to give forgiveness.

I still hungered for my son's murderer to experience firsthand the full magnitude of the injury done to me and my family. I needed him to accept the wrongness of his actions and feel the anguish of remorse for taking these lives.

I wanted him to fear his own death and know that no blood sacrifice on any altar would release him from his fate, but I knew I was not the one to bring him to this dark knowledge.

Most importantly, I had to let anger burn in me for a time before I could let it go.

Anger Burning Cold

My anger, once so hot, burns colder now
My all-consuming, blinding red rage banked, focused
turned outward with laser intensity

aching to pierce the heart of my son's murderer

I slowly accept that it is not my right, not my due
I burn past the insanity of vengeance, past the lust for blood
past my hunger to rend his flesh and smear his blood

to cause him pain

to make him feel that lightning moment
when he knows his life ends now
that he will live no more

When disbelief turns to terror

When that moment, that awful knowledge his life is over
becomes his universe

That moment my son knew

That shrieking moment when he cowers in terror
unable to cheat his fate, unable to quench my fury
that instant when he knows his doom

That madness has passed me now
replaced with a hunger for justice
a need to see this man punished, to hear his actions condemned

as he has condemned me to live this life of pain
of lost hopes, lost futures
to wander forever without the touch of my son

the embrace of his love

Much harder to accept the necessity to forgive
to embrace instead he who caused me so much pain and loss
to let this anger burn cold lest it consume my soul

but not now, it is still too soon

let me hold the flame for a little while longer
keep the anger close to warm my frozen heart
in the middle of the night

and dream red dreams

~

Forgiveness is Hard

Hatred bloomed in me for a time. I hated that young man. I hated Antwan's family and wanted them to suffer the same loss that I had. I felt my humanity slipping away from me. My hatred ran unchecked for a while.

I watched his grandparents during the trial. They raised him because his crack addict mother was not around. His lover was there too, dressed in a bizarre mixture of street tough and pop singer glamour. I listened closely to every point the prosecutor made and my hatred deepened.

It was clear from the disrespect and distain the defendant showed to the court, and everyone present, that he was not going to accept responsibility for the killings. He showed no remorse for his casual destruction of so many lives. None of the testimony moved him in the slightest. No trace of humanity ever flitted across his iron visage. Not even when they showed the most damming and hurtful piece of evidence.

The defense attorney tried to make the point that Aaron and Jacob were not wearing seat belts when they were hit, suggesting their neglect contributed to their deaths. To refute this, the prosecution displayed photographs of my two dead boys bodies clearly showing slanted bruises across their chests formed when the seat belts held them in place as the car crushed them.

Everyone was stunned, and I couldn't hold back my wail of grief. I felt that I was being forced down onto the bench seat by that same crushing blow. It felt like a hot blast of air roared over me, raising sweat all over my body. My face was on fire and it felt like fire ants were biting me everywhere. They quickly turned off the projector and called a recess. I couldn't stand up and had to stay put until I cooled down. I was enraged and nothing could stem the feelings of hate flooding from my broken heart.

That moment was hard to endure and I have been trying to put other pictures of Aaron in my mind ever since. Try as I must, that image keeps returning to tear at me. That was my worst moment in that courtroom. As the trial progressed, I saw how my anger was changing me. I was becoming someone I would not be able to live with.

Eventually, I felt my humanity return. I saw the pain Antwan's grandparents were experiencing as his actions were exposed to the court. I heard his cross gender lover blame himself for not being able to keep Antwan at home that night. I started to feel a pain that was not my own. I could hardly contain my own pain, much less feel theirs, but I could not stem the flow of their anguish into me.

The impact of their pain broke the vicious hold that anger and hatred held on my heart, and I felt compassion for their suffering. There were no winners in that court, only losers. We were all facing unfathomable loss. We were all fellow sufferers.

I found myself approaching the grandparents at a break in the trial, and somehow we all started praying as the tears fell unchecked. I found a strange peace in those prayers and knew I would have to find forgiveness for the man who murdered my son Aaron and his partner Jacob. Not for his sake but for mine.

The young man's lover came over and joined us, and I told him that he was not responsible for the darkness done that night. He held no blame and could not be allowed to borrow guilt that wasn't his.

I could not hold that hatred in my heart anymore. I wrote *Forgiveness is Hard* as a way to understand and wrestle with the forces that held me in my hatred. The forces that that were tearing at me and threatened to consume me. It is my promise. Someday—I must forgive.

Forgiveness is Hard

It's easier to give up vengeance than to give forgiveness
I pretend to be civilized
just enough to forgo my hot mad rage for revenge

I can get past vengeance—anger lingers longer, lives deeper

The outrage, the pain
the deep sharp bone scraping pain I endure daily
feeds my anger

the ache to destroy the one who has in turn destroyed our lives
can be assuaged by justice
satisfied somewhat in the process of punishment

But forgiveness

To forgive, I must finally put aside my anger
I must look deep within to see humanity in the killer
I must embrace the source of pain

I must draw him close and believe his sins can be absolved
It feels so dishonest, a disservice to my lost one
it feels a betrayal to his memory

I want that aching loss
that ripped out piece of my heart to count for something more
So I find it hard to let go of my anger

to move forward into forgiveness

All our cultures, all our religions, teach the necessity of forgiveness

that God forgives everything:
even the burning of Jews

even the slaughter of Cambodian babies
even public executions of Islamic women
all of these things God forgives, and more. Must we too?

Is God driven by cosmic indifference or deep divine love?

I understand neither, both lie beyond comprehension
my capacity to embrace
but still I must face the need to forgive. I kneel bereft of grace

I try—but fall so short

Still my anger consumes me, blinds me to the path
to my forgiveness. I lack the compassion
I fear I will be left empty if I give up my anger, and forgive

But more, I fear the waste

I fear my awful sacrifice, my betrayal of sacred memory
the action that will tear so deeply at my soul
will mean nothing to the one forgiven

Who sits uncaring
locked in the iron machine of captivity
unwilling to show emotion that might show weakness

afraid to lose face
to diminish his position
in the rabid dog food chain of prison

Who sits unmoving, unmoved
face a frozen mask, unable to meet my eye
I pour this gentle gift of forgiveness on him

only to see it fall unheeded to the floor

to be walked on, spat on, ignored
but noticed perhaps by God
who might in turn forgive me

Finally

I slowly learn
Forgiveness is not for the forgiven
but for the soul of the forgiver

Forgiveness is hard, but still it must be done
to release my soul from this unending spiral of grief
I must believe that even this one can be saved

even this one may someday touch God
even this one I must forgive
Even with my son torn bleeding from my heart

I must forgive

~

Chapter Five

Poems of Bargaining

bargaining with fate
take my sacrifice in trade
powerless I grieve

There are times when the pain, and suffering, of grief can become so hard to bear that we look for any means to reverse our loss. When grieving loss, we pull out everything we have ever learned to cope with our emotions. Bargaining is itself a respite from pain. One more distraction that lets us focus on something else so the pain can be put aside for a little time.

When we are children we learn to bargain early, enhancing our limited power when dealing with the world around us. We negotiate our treats and duties with our parents and ask our playmates for do-over's when the game goes against us. We carry those skills into adulthood and refine them.

Bargaining with fate gives us the illusion we have power over it. That we can actually change things that are unchangeable. We imagine we have more power that we really do, and that can backfire on us and feed our feelings of guilt. We try to bargain but find we are now faced with events that cannot be negotiated away.

My bargaining led me to pray to God to take my life as a sacrifice and release my son. I wished with all my heart that I could have taken his place at that blinding moment and died instead of him. I felt the soul bite of survivor's guilt. As I explained earlier, guilt has no long term use and can only bring harm to us and the ones who care about us. I eventually learned I could no longer let lingering guilt constrain or direct my actions.

I recall clearly one intense act of bargaining two months after my son died. I was driving to work, and a vision of the moment of his death overcame me. The vision was so strong that I had to pull over to the side of the road so I wouldn't hit anyone. I felt his agony and despair, and was desperate to help him. I tried to project myself into that space as the car collapsed around him and his partner.

I wanted to be the victim instead of him, but I couldn't make that happen. I remember that the feeling of loss was so extreme that I didn't know how I could continue. The guilt I felt at my perceived failure lingered longer. That vision haunted me, repeating at odd intervals. Each time I had to fight off feelings of guilt that I knew could only bring me more pain.

I finally came to terms with these episodes when, during the trial, the County coroner testified that the crash happened so fast that Aaron and Jacob must have died instantly. I held on to that cold comfort for a long time.

Calculus of Loss

I was realizing the futility of bargaining when I wrote *Calculus of Loss.* I wanted that terrible moment erased, so I could regain the life I had before.

I wanted just one more chance to see Aaron again, to talk to him, to hold him a last time. I wanted the pain to stop for just a little while. I wanted my do-over. Oh God—I wanted my do-over, but I was no longer a child.

Calculus of Loss

Of what worth is a hug? How much for a kiss?

It used to cost a buck
to kiss a pretty cheerleader
in a kissing booth

Aren't kisses from one you love worth more?

How much do we add for the *last* kiss?
How much would you pay for one *more* kiss
one *more* hug,when the source is forever lost?

Money?—Useless
Jewelry, precious objects?—Worthless
No matter how dear

Could we pay perhaps with a piece of our soul?

A bit of essence we would gladly trade
for just one touch

A little life for just one kiss
just another moment together

Can we work that trade with God?
Is she listening? Can you hear me?

No
Silence reigns
Deal denied

Signal lost and gone forever

There will be no more kisses
no more hugs
no matter how much we would pay

We can only wrap ourselves in memories
hug them tight, kiss another in their name
Reach out in the dark to bring them close

whisper love from soul to soul
The cost?—Only pain. Loss made real
The return?—A bit of solace

A little lessening of grief

A moment joined to savor shared joys
shared triumphs, shared hurts
those very inside jokes

The minutiae of a shared life
important to only us
Wondrous return at such a little cost

A hug is worth our world if we could but buy it

~

Double Vision

Double Vision shows how early bargaining can come to us in grief. I wrote it just after my son's funeral to capture how I felt when I looked in his coffin. I know it is a difficult poem to read, as it was to write, but I urge you to read it nonetheless. It is an intimate look at my soul laid bare at the nadir of my life. I felt my own death at that moment and tried a father's ancient bargain with his God.

I begged that I be allowed to be the one in the coffin and my son the viewer. I felt so clearly that was the way it should have been, but I was forced to endure this bizarre reversal of fate. He should be going on to fulfill all those promises and I to fade away. He should be writing these words instead of me. Ah, but he and I have conspired to thwart fate. As I sit here writing, I feel his presence inside of me guiding my prose as well as my poetry. Father and son, of one mind.

Double Vision

I stand alone at my son's coffin
eyes fixed on his cold powdered face
The sweet sick scent of lilies

claw the inside of my nose

Shaking, I grip the cushioned sides
afraid to touch his precious skin
alien now with death

The cherished body I held from birth
and tired to keep from harm
broken

The Hammer of death
pounds my flesh
driving me to my knees

Air grinds through my teeth
I shrink within myself
compacting to a leaden knot of pain

My head turns slowly from the box
a groan escapes
from deep inside me

enormous gravity forces me down
plummeting into a void
Life forced out to match the death before me

My mind is cleft in two

one part caught in fire
raging and devastated

one part coolly detached
displaced and dispassioned

An inner voice
slices through the crash of grief

A bizarre critic
analyzing my every action

Get off your knees
Don't make a scene
You sound like some demented Wooky

Shut Up!
Stop it!
Stand up and face it you coward!

Cruel commands tear me

forcing awareness of my insignificance
before this massive reality

Who am I to grieve when my son lies breathless?
How dare I wallow in display while my son rots?

My trickster mind
desperate to avoid pain
to avoid madness

Terrified by evidence of its own mortality
denies my son is gone
and so will I also be

Some time, some way
perhaps in this very room
In a box like this—gone

What selfish selfness permits me
to see my own face in the box
replacing that of my son?

To see my death instead of his?
Selfish thinking or wishful thinking?
A father's ancient bargain with his god

Before I can answer
my mind crashes together
back into a fused mass of misfiring neurons

Gentle hands raise me up
lead me away in a fog of confusion
through a wavering blur of tears

Stunned by the magnitude of loss

~

Chapter Six

Poems of Depression

numb—I face the dawn
another day locked in grief
despair fogs the light

Unlike the single repeated note of clinical depression, I experienced many of the other emotional states while in still immersed in my feelings of depression. Depression was like walking in a fog. I would often emerge from the gloom to find a little happiness, or to spend some time in restful reflection of the progress of my growing acceptance. Sometimes I would lose myself in warm and comforting memories of the precious moments Aaron and I shared.

Depression is considered to be a stage of grief, but my experience was that depression underlies all the other stages. How could I respond to this loss and not feel depressed? Along with sorrow, depression was the most prevalent emotion I experienced. I believe the transient, and ever changing feelings of sadness and depression, were a natural response to my very real pain. These feelings lessened in intensity as I gained acceptance, and came to terms with my loss.

While still in a state of deep depression, I was driving home from work and started to feel pains in my chest. My hands were tingling, and I found it difficult to breathe. I thought I was having a heart attack.

I pulled over to the side of the road and turned off the engine. I didn't feel like going any further. I thought—perhaps this is a good time to leave. I was strangely calm when I realized I just didn't care anymore.

The magnitude of my loss overwhelmed me, like so many things overwhelmed me in those days. I sat and waited for it all to end. After a while, I realized that the feelings had passed. The pain had left my chest, but my hands were still tingling. I thought perhaps it would be safe to drive, so I went back to my house and told Lisa what happened. She became very upset and called my doctor.

We were told to go to the emergency room and ask to have me admitted immediately. When we arrived, the nurses rushed me to a bed and hooked a bunch of wires onto me. I told the panicky young doctor who was attending that I thought I had suffered a heart attack. She yelled at me, "You are having a heart attack right now!" For some reason, this amused me. All this fuss, and I couldn't care less.

My depression had crept up on me and was smothering my will to live. I had been doing so well after my Dark Night that I didn't think I would have this kind of problem. The anger and bargaining hadn't helped me, and I felt so helpless after putting out all that fruitless energy. Everything seemed so futile and meaningless.

It later turned out that I hadn't had a heart attack after all. It was just an extreme form of stress that caused my sternum to spasm, simulating a heart attack. The massive amounts of stress poison, still pumping through my body from all my anger, probably didn't help either. I felt weak and powerless.

What shook me most about this whole episode was my placid acceptance of death. This shock me made me face the truth that I wanted to live after all. I was struggling hard to overcome my depression, but it seemed so difficult in the middle of it.

I now understand that in extreme cases of grief, where the loss is a unexpected or violent, grief lasts much longer. Experts call this a complicated grief. Denial is much stronger, anger more intense, sadness and depression are felt much deeper. Acceptance is hard to achieve, and harder to hold onto. I eventually learned to deal with even these strong emotions, and continue my healing. The resolution and comfort of my acceptance was drawing ever closer. I just needed to keep moving forward along my path, enduring grief with each step.

Living with Echoes

I started to become aware of the 'ghosts' surrounding me, and wrote *Living with Echoes*. I experienced the death of several people who were close to me in a short period of time and still felt their presence near to me. Rather than having spooky feelings, I felt warm comfort in our continuing, albeit quiet, relationships.

The memories of our closeness and interaction seemed to walk into the future with me. How could they be truly gone if I could remember them? The 'ghosts' were just echoes of passed lives. Their memories seemed to still resonate within me, fresh and near. I could not forget them as long as I drew breath.

Living with Echoes

I look at the empty spot on the stairs
a step half way up
at just eye level

where my old cat Satchmo used to sit

His favorite perch
he could watch the room
bat people when they passed by

Satchmo, the kitten with the gravelly voice
grown to a tired old gentleman
sitting on the step where he could look you in the eyes

to remind you it was he who ruled this house

he who kept you safe from crickets

I look at the place where my mother used to sit
where she would spin fantastic stories of family exploits
perhaps true, perhaps not, but always enthralling

Sometimes I would find outside information to prove her stories
incredible as they may have been
but now she is gone—apart but still loved

Then I look at the place my son used to sit, close to me
where we would engage in our many "discussions"
energetic arguments, just this side of a fight

We talked about all those difficult subjects:
religion, politics, sexuality, man's inhumanity to man
the big issues, the ones that strike deep

He would lean back in deceptive languor
legs stretched out
arms crossed over the top of his head, airing his armpits

eyes half shut
intent glare peeping out beneath his lids
aping my own position

Then jerk forward suddenly
intent, impassioned
eyes blazing fiercely

his whole body arrested in forward thrust
ready to leap to his feet, to underline his point
brilliance blazing forth

All of them gone now
but I feel them still so close
I hear softly whispered advice

for the things I do, the choices I must make
I need, and heed, I follow their guidance
tap their courage, share their wisdom

My son still close to me when I write
helps me craft the right phrase
keeps me honest, makes me tell the truth

forcing me to dig deep
to wrestle with the difficult subjects
the ones we met with such passion

to capture the emotions that drive us
the things that pull our hearts, and choke our throats
the moments, events and memories

that bring us tears

I sit at night, alone
next to his empty chair
Our arguments echo in memory

our discussions continue
he a bit less vocal
but still speaking clearly

my God—I miss him

I walk past the stairs
and a ghostly paw bats softly at my head
just above my ear

Satchmo letting me know he still is there
still guarding the house, keeping watch
hunting crickets

I hear my mom's stories
weaving the fabric of our family
reminding me of past accomplishments

urging me to walk new paths
to discover new truths
craft the substance of new stories

I listen to my son
who still plays little tricks on me
perhaps it is just my distracted mind

I hear him clearly
urging me to keep it real, to stay with the truth
ignore the pain and bare my soul to you

to let you know the ghosts we walk with
the whispers we hear in the dark
are just echoes of passed lives

words that resonate deep within
reflections that vibrate deep in our souls
precious memories

that keep them alive, fresh, and near

~

Waking to Loss

It was hard to return to work while still grieving heavily. Just getting through the day seemed to be an overwhelming act of bravery. I learned to set my sights lower than before and not judge myself.

Sometimes I only had the strength to walk through the door and declare victory. Anything I accomplished after that was a bonus.

Depression brought me a mixed sense of distance, confusion and numbness. This is what I was feeling when I wrote *Waking to Loss*. Sometimes I would sleepwalk through my day and then jump at an imagined shadow at the edge of my vision. I found this disconnectedness from reality passed as I kept doggedly plodding forward.

Waking to Loss

Each night I collapse into sleep
only to rise restless
dreamless, unsatisfied

No gradual upward float from dark
no comfortable rise from mist
no easy gathering of thought

just up with a start

Reality crashes into waking consciousness
memories that lay waiting for awareness to stir
vanish sleep with the flash of fact

my son is dead.

I try to dodge, return to oblivion, hide from the real
but find myself fixed, arrested
stabbed through by this spear of truth

I walk in shock
clothed in numbness
trying to accept the knowledge of death

Unwilling to face a world without him
unable to perform the necessities of life
but forced by circumstance to continue

I try to do the simple tasks
to slide through morning routine
carry out motions engrained by years of repetition

only to stand befuddled
overwhelmed with uncertainty
unsure how to proceed

Lost for a while
mind wheeling unconnected
transfixed by shadows in the mirror

I jump, jerk in response to movement
glimpsed at the edge of vision
I turn to find nothing, no source of motion

no thing to trigger my sudden fright

I move through the day distracted
movements unresponsive to my needs

The phone rings and I answer the remote control
I stop in confusion
puzzled by an unfamiliar pattern of buttons

My memory betrays me
I start to call out
driven by the need to share a thought

to ask some advice
to see how he's doing
and then I remember

loss drives deep inside me, crushing
forcing out the fog of forgetfulness
I return again to grief, continue the cycle

adding layers to the growing pearl of my acceptance

~

Sick Again

The poisonous chemicals my body released daily in response to the physical exertions, and emotional upheavals, of grief took a heavy toll on my health and immune system. My nervous system went into a prolonged stress mode, pouring 'flight or fight' hormones and steroids into my body that weakened my ability to fight off infections. One cold seemed to chase another, and the pervasive symptoms just underlined the pain in my suffering. I was sick within and without.

One interminable night, five months into my grieving, I surrendered to insomnia and arose to write *Sick Again*. The little miseries of my colds were magnified by the night. Sleep kept slipping farther away from me, and I had the shrinking feeling I was losing yet another chance to recover. I knew the hour was fast approaching when I had to leave my bed and face another day, stumbling and sneezing down my path through grief.

Sick Again

Eyes half closed—puffed and streaming
muscles aching—head pounding
nose and sinus blocked—ears clogged and chest heavy

I shiver my way through the third cold in as many months

Brief respites between attacks
serve only to punctuate
the lingering hours of my suffering

Immune system laid low, body open to marauding viral hordes

random infections
dust and pollen's sting
the hungry bite of bacteria

all defenses compromised by the relentless stress poison of grief

I knew the toll
the grind of grief
would take on my soul

sit astonished at how deeply it attacks my body

scrambling messages
throwing me off balance
shattering my equilibrium

I add chemicals, bitter potions and herbs
to boost my waning defenses

fighting to lessen little miseries
ease my breathing
stifle coughing jags

dry my weeping eyes
and capture the healing release of sleep

I try vainly throughout the night
to slip the tenacious tethers of fretful consciousness
and halt the grim remembering

embrace the little death of thought
and float in blissful forgetfulness

But the wheezing in my chest
the clotting in my craw
the wracking coughs that shake me, rasp my throat

and spark random lights that dance in the dark

to the pounding in my head
all conspire to deny me surcease
force me to dwell in my memories

and contemplate again the immense magnitude of my loss

All thoughts of release fled
I walk once more the paths of pain and acceptance
Until wearily, I sink exhausted into a troubled and restless sleep

Slowly healing—each troubled breath wearily following the last

~

Quaking

Near the end of the major part of my depression, I wrote *Quaking*. The deadening feelings of depression pulled me inward, distracting me from my seemingly endless world of emotions.

I gained time to rest, for a while, from the sharpness of my painful periods of mourning. I still had the meltdowns, but they were somewhat muted. Loss in a minor chord.

When the grieving cycles resumed, and the sharp pain of loss returned to me, I found my body shaking in the extremity of my sorrow, but I had gained the strength to endure them again.

Quaking

I wake to the thin grey light of dawn
watching colors slowly emerge
in a room still cloaked in shadow

Encased in my translucent shell of porcelain silence

I strive to lie motionless so as not to disturb my sleeping wife
Exhausted by grief she twists fitfully in a troubled dream
cheeks rimed with salt, the mark of tears shed openly in the dark

Grief blooms within, pressing my aching and clenched throat
I clamp down hard, squeezing back a treacherous sob
determined to stay still, quiet, contained, unmoved

An inexorable pressure builds within me, seeking escape
Denied its normal path, it skitters desperately to find release
tearing, shredding, scattering my resolve

I fight back vainly with a wavering will
pull my sinews up tight, grit my teeth
refuse to submit—and am undone

A slow quavering starts in the muscles of my chest
a strange vibration beating time to the rhythm of my heart
driven by the tension of my trapped emotions

It grows, spreads outward
seizes my body in its unyielding grasp
and breaks free

unleashing a terrible shaking in my limbs
twitching my face, shivering my soul
I lie quaking with abandon in the growing light

Quivering without restraint
caught in agony
unable to escape

lost in emotion close to ecstasy
close to agape, closer to terror
straining with every fiber of my being to break free

Trapped and impotent in a new and humbling form of grief

~

Prayer from Despair

I found the first three lines of *Prayer from Despair* in fragments of my son's writing. Aaron visited the site of the Oklahoma City bombing of 1995 and captured his impressions in a notebook. This poem is a blend of both of us.

I remember praying to find a bit of comfort in the midst of all my pain. I was also spending a lot of time contemplating my shadow self, and working to reclaim the gifts hidden inside me. I learned to embrace every moment of my life and accept whatever comes to me with gratitude.

All my experiences, good and bad, served to make me who I am. I find that I really like who I have become. Did I mention that my son was a teacher? Now he teaches me how to walk through my grief; he steadies me when I stumble.

Prayer from Despair

Beloved Creator
help me find the grace to continue
when my path is dim and hard to walk

and the weight of loss too heavy to bear alone
Help me to move past pain and fear
and grow in understanding and acceptance

When grief swells in my chest
and shivers deep inside me
help me to find joy in the heart of sorrow

Help me to find the gifts
hidden within dark memories of the past
and the strength to let those memories go

Let me embrace every moment of my life
with equal grace
filled with gratitude for the solace of

Your unconditional love

Chapter Seven

Poems of Acceptance

rapt in acceptance
awake to eternity
living love anew

Eventually I gained an increasing acceptance of my loss, but I never stopped missing, or thinking about, my son. He was gone, and I will forever want him back. Grief permanently changed me. I gradually accepted my loss and adjusted my life to accommodate this hard truth. I found acceptance several times during my years of grieving, and each time that acceptance deepened.

> *The reality is that you will grieve forever. You will not 'get over' the loss of a loved one; you will learn to live with it. You will heal, and you will rebuild yourself around the loss you have suffered. You will be whole again, but you will never be the same. Nor should you be the same, nor would you want to.*
>
> Elisabeth Kübler-Ross

I found that acceptance is not an event but a process. My initial acceptance of the reality of my loss was only the beginning. I had to accept my loss, understand the full impact of the loss on me, understand how to adjust my life to live in a world without my son. I then had to accept my changed world.

The process of understanding and acceptance took time, and was guided by the experience and expression of my grief. My current state of acceptance was built from growing layers of interim acceptance resulting from my cyclic episodes of grieving.

These episodes were punctuated by meltdowns followed by periods of healing. The healing led to a deepening of my understanding, adjustment, and growing acceptance.

Mars Meets the Moon

I found my first act of acceptance, just weeks after Aaron's death, while sitting in a little Santa Barbara garden. I wrote this piece before I discovered the need to write poetry.

In early September of 2003, Mars was closer to the Earth than it had been in thousands of years and would look like a bright red star passing behind the Moon in the night sky. I was still stunned by the magnitude of my loss, and I was fighting desperately for some way to understand the new terrain I had been thrust into. Nothing made sense to me anymore. I felt all my faith slipping away, like sand under my feet, as I trudged along the shore of an immense ocean of grief.

The burial service for my son was still fresh in my mind, and I kept hearing the hymn they sang for him, *In the Garden*. I tried to sing it myself, but my emotions would overwhelm me before I could finish any of the verses. I confess that my throat still tightens when I sing it.

The hymn was written by a minister who was mourning the loss of his beloved. I knew Aaron would have loved to hear me sing it, but I thought he was forever beyond the reach of my voice. I sat in the dark, watching distant wanderers move to touch in the sky. I felt a presence grow close. I met my son that night in the little garden and gained a small measure of solace as he walked with me into my dark new world.

I sang for him then, just a little, as much as my heart could bear.

Mars Meets the Moon

I went to the garden alone tonight and watched Mars rise. The blood red wanderer passing close to the Earth outshone only by a gibbous Moon

I went to the garden alone to mourn the recent passing of my son. My wife, Lisa, and I are in the darkest place we have ever been since we met at Venice High in 1967. The Summer of Love.

I sat in the garden alone staring into darkness. Mars embraced the Moon. I embraced my loss. The universe started to balance.

I wept in the garden alone and sang softly to my son the old spiritual we sung at his funeral. I sang while he sat quietly with me and held me in my grief.

He walked with me, and he talked with me, and he told me I was his own. As we tarried there …

I still grieve, but this special place is helping me take the first steps to healing. Lisa tells me that we will never get over this, but we will get through it.

I need to walk with Lisa in this garden and help her universe balance. May god hold you in his arms. Blessed Be, Mijo.

Closure Myth

Three years after my son's death, I wrote about the gradual growth of my acceptance in my poem, *Closure Myth.* I don't think you ever get closure when you lose a child. I admit that, after almost eight years, I am still not done with grief. However; I am coping with his death much better and have gained a great deal of understanding, and acceptance, of my loss. I used grief to completely transform my life and found a level of happiness and personal satisfaction that I never knew existed.

I learned to love and treasure myself, and have learned to share great love with others. In spite of all my successes, I still feel grief. I probably always will, but grief falls much lighter on me now. I watch a sappy movie and get overcome by emotions, both good and bad. I hear a story, or watch a movie, where a child dies, and I find myself pounding my chest and rocking in my chair while suffering a deep stab of pain in my heart. These episodes soon pass, but they are still deeply felt.

I can't 'just get over it', as several well meaning people have urged me to do. Closure for me is a myth, but I have learned to accept my changed life. I even realize how much better my life is now, not from the loss, but from my response to it. Just as an oyster wraps nacre around an irremovable intrusion of alien matter, understanding, won from the soul agony of grief, wrapped layers of acceptance around the intrusion of my loss.

In this poem I break the 'Fourth Wall' and speak directly to you. I ask if my words touch you because I deeply want to touch you with this knowledge. From that place of pain inside me, I speak to that place of pain inside you.

I ask you to accept the pain of grief, and learn to understand and accept your loss. I ask you to be gentle with yourself, and let the natural healing of sorrow flow through you. Don't spare the tears, and ignore anyone who would tell you how to grieve. Your grief is your own and unlike anyone else's. Trust yourself to find your own way to acceptance at your own pace. I don't presume to give you a checklist, or a schedule, for grief. I can only pass on advice based on what I have experienced myself.

I do ask you, while you are searching within, to be open to discoveries of how wonderful a being you truly are. Don't shrink from your brilliance. Look unflinchingly at your life, and search for anything that might hold you back from fully experiencing happiness. Happiness is your due by virtue of your existence. Existence springs from, and continues to be, an act of love. Embrace your future with your entire being, and accept your place in it. You will find solace in the love you shared, and continue to share, with your lost one. You will find joy in others when you open your life to them again. There is joy at the heart of sorrow. I found it and know it is there for you. Just open yourself and accept it.

Closure Myth

There is no closure, only layers of acceptance
built slowly by the groping of a befuddled mind
shocked by the cold reality of pain and loss

Soul's agony wrapped in the nacre of understanding

I shrink from asking if you enjoy my words, the work that flows
to fill the emptiness within with meaning and form
That aching space from whence love and logic has fled

Better I should ask; do they touch you?

Do you share my struggle to release the binds
the buried tethers of memory and emotion?
Dusty hurts and ancient cuts that still spark fear

blinding us to our own true brilliance

I strain to release that long trapped grief

Embrace the pain and find the lessons locked within
Use this harsh teaching to accept loss and continue life

No closure, only layers of acceptance

We cannot just get over grief, but we can get through it
with changed beliefs, new depths of compassion
a truer love for the brief sweet joy of life

Grateful for our now, the moments of our shared existence

~

Hyper Vigilance

I wrote *Hyper Vigilance* when I finally figured out why I was watching for any sign that my son might have, somehow, returned. I would walk into a room, fully expecting to see him, only to be frustrated. I kept seeing shadows moving just at the edges of my vision and would whirl to meet them finding nothing.

I asked my therapist about this behavior, and she said it was called Hyper Vigilance. I was on alert and could not come down from that state. I didn't trust reality; I kept my eye on it.

I was constantly searching for any threat to my family, so I could rush to protect them. I felt that I had let down my guard once, with terrible consequences, and would not let that happen again.

I see now, I was trying to understand how these events had occurred and was finally coming to terms with my loss. I was feeling a deep guilt at my failure to prevent my son's death and could not find a way to let go of my perceived guilt. I saw myself as a sentry who fell asleep at my post.

I learned long ago the severe penalty for losing vigilance, and now I was paying the harshest penalty I could imagine. It took time to let go of that guilt, but I finally figured out that there was nothing I could have done to change events. I did not fall asleep at my post. I could stand down.

Hyper Vigilance

I never used to startle so easily
jumping at shadows, jerking around at strange sounds
flinching at imaginary movements, just out of view

I find myself obsessed with every little change in my surroundings
no matter how minute, how seemingly inconsequential
ever since the universe failed me

I wait and watch for any change that could be a threat
to me, to my family, to the ones I love

I will not allow the world to harvest
another soul from under my care without a fight

I will not be fooled again

lulled into complacency by my perceptions
blinded by my beliefs, distracted by my conviction

that everything happens for a reason

I know now the casual cruelty
of a harsh and brutish reality

How quickly random chance
could snuff out the life of my cherished one

How fast that vital essence was snatched from my grasp

love lost forever

How the axis of my world could shift with terrible finality
in an instant

I know now, no matter how we pray
to whatever deity we revere
to whatever we hold sacred

to whatever entity of illusion in which we place our trust
no matter how we try to bargain
with whatever we hold dear

that fateful moment that craves denial
remains undeniable

That little slip of time
we strive with forlorn hope to change
remains unchangeable

Reality remains immutable

We cannot regain that which is lost
cannot bend the rules to lessen our grief
cannot fill that aching void

where our hearts used to beat

We can only endure, struggle for understanding
search for a way to accept
a colder, emptier, existence

One without the touch
the warm comforting embrace
we yearn for

The one in which we will live whatever life is left to us

and watch with unceasing vigilance
the assaults of an uncaring world

until slowly, painfully, we once more learn to trust

~

I see the start of my grudging acceptance in this poem for a reality I didn't wish for, or want, but one that I must accept and live in. My hyper vigilance finally faded, as my acceptance grew. Slowly, painfully, I once more learned to trust.

Taking Care

Part of my acceptance was to adapt myself to the new world I was facing. Grief took a toll on my body and my mind. Stress poisons compromised my immune system, and I forgot to take care of myself. I wrote *Taking Care* when I realized that I finally cared about my battered body.

I used to procrastinate, feeling that I had all the time in the world. I could no longer hide behind that fantasy. The sudden nature of my son's death taught me to pay attention to today, because it might be my last day of life. I was faced with my physical mess and it bothered me.

I needed to live a better and healthier life. I believed that whatever was left of his memories, his remaining contact with me, were contained in this body of mine. I didn't want it to be the physical wreck I saw in the mirror.

I wanted to live, and I wanted to live well. I got to work and rebuilt my physical self, while my mind was rebuilding my mental self. My heart was healing.

Taking Care

Grunting at my Soloflex in the thin morning light
disturbing dust slowly deposited since 9/11
that other day when reality stuttered

Carpe Diem lessons driven deep by the death of my boy
"time's winged chariot hurrying near"
drives my will to progress

to move forward into a world forever changed

Straining and squeezing tired muscles
unaccustomed to the rhythmic strain
protesting each new push against resisting mass

fighting gravity and time
punishing and pushing
a slow improvement of myself

He used to despair
at my casual disregard for my appearance
Outdated and worn clothes

scuffed shoes, ragged nails, shaggy hair
"Da-ad, you don't *have* to be gay to look good
you hetros can show some style too."

Now, too late, I strive to change, to upgrade my image
to improve my act, to be worthy of his memory
and finally learn those lessons he tried to teach

I try to rebuild, take better care of myself
reverse somewhat
the tattering grind of time

I look at buffed nails on manicured hands
so different from their normal state
but times are no longer normal

Reality changed, if only for my little world
I wear designer tee shirts to bed
drink protein shakes for breakfast, chew salad for lunch

no longer living with the assumption
that tomorrow is soon enough
Tomorrow might be a myth, unattainable

a wisp I may never catch

So I live in the now, and love in the now
and miss him now
as I will miss him for the rest of my days

I cherish each new dawn
accept each new gift of existence
fill each precious day

with all the meaning and joy
I can bring myself to create
I live each day as my last, as that last day was for him

Each day above the ground a victory

UNDER THE SAMHAIN MOON

A few years after I lost Aaron, I was missing him a lot during the Halloween season. I remembered dressing Aaron, and his twin sister Anna-Lisa, in costumes and taking them out for trick or treat. We would dare the night armed with flashlights and prowl the walkway streets of Venice, California, searching for tasty treasure. On our return home, we would dump all the treats on the carpet in the living room so I could examine them for anything unusual.

There were rumors of people putting dangerous things in the candy, and I wanted to be careful. I told the twins I was checking it out to make sure it was good candy. We split the haul between them, so there would be no hard feelings.

It's very important to keep everything equal between children, especially twins. I let them eat what they wanted right then, and we put the candy away, to be doled out over the next few months. I loved those memories and wanted to relive those lost days.

I was raised Catholic with a deep spiritual view of Halloween. I grew up in a community containing several families with a strong Mexican heritage, who honored that time of the year as the day of the dead, *Dia de Los Muertos*. As a result, I always viewed Halloween as a time to pray for the dead and welcome them among the living for a while.

I later learned that Halloween was based on the Celtic festival of Samhain. The traditional Celtic view is that the membrane between the living and the dead is thinnest during that night, so it is easier for the living to invite the dead in to visit. I didn't see this as morbid but rather a way to share one more moment with my lost one.

I hungered for that moment with all my being, so I lit a candle and turned off all the lights in the house. I sat for a while in the dark and waited. I used to be afraid of the dark, but there was nothing to fear that night. I recalled all the good times we shared on those cherished Halloween nights. I remembered our adventures running from house to house in the dark with all the other families, and I could see again the excitement on all those little faces when they received their treats.

Slowly, I started to relax and felt joy rising up from within. I could feel a happiness that had been missing from my heart for so long, and I imagined I could feel his laughter filling the void within me. I felt him draw close to me that night, and the love we once shared returned to me.

I was so happy for those few minutes that I didn't care if I was imagining his closeness; it didn't matter if I was living in a gentle delusion. He was there, he was close to me for a time, and that's all that mattered. I drew comfort from those minutes I shared with his memory. It was a time of healing that I needed.

Oh yeah—in the haiku—the bit about the shave. Aaron and I share a common affliction. We both have a tough beard, growing from a tender skin, so shaving is always a trial. I solved the problem by growing a beard, but Aaron felt a full beard made him look too old. He was also researching the life of Kurt Cobain for a book he was writing and liked the grunge look.

I used to kid him about his three day old beard and loved it when he hugged me and scratched my cheek with it. I needed to feel that scratchy cheek pressed against mine. Now I can feel it whenever I read this little haiku.

Under the Samhain Moon

LifeDeath's membrane thins
his lips brush my upturned face
he still needs a shave

~

THE CHECK

I have to admit that I didn't want to reveal what I wrote in *The Check.* I felt strong guilt over my actions, so I kept the poem hidden. I decided to share it, because it taught me a valuable lesson about anger and guilt.

After my Aaron's death I had to pack up the things in his apartment and move them to my house. I found piles of unopened mail containing a lot of unpaid bills. It was difficult to contact his creditors and tell them that he was dead, but I had to do it. I found several debts that I had co-signed, so I made arrangements for payment. Many of these debts were past due and had to be paid immediately. I had just finished paying for the funeral, so I was a bit overextended financially. It was hard to deal with debt in the midst of grieving. In desperation, I called his employer to see if he had taken out a life insurance policy. He had, but they would not tell me who the beneficiary was.

I remember getting very angry about this and felt betrayed that he left me all these debts and forgot to name a beneficiary for his insurance policy. Perhaps he left his money to someone else. My anger was unreasonable, but I felt it all the same. I was consumed by my anger and directed it at him. This caused me to feel great guilt over my anger. The angrier I got, the more guilt I felt. I seemed to be spiraling down into a disturbing kind of depression.

Then, I got a check in the mail. I was stunned and then shamed by all my raging. He had left the money to his mother and me after all. I felt an overwhelming guilt for my anger at him, and for acting so badly. I wrestled with my guilt and felt it dissipate.

Depression gave way to the introspection of sorrow, and I started to understand what had really happened. He was focused on his true purpose in life, taking care of what was important, and all the little details of life would have to wait until he could deal with them. With this perspective, I was able to write *The Check* to capture my feelings, and my understanding of this experience. I never wanted to forget what I learned from such pain.

When we are locked in the immense stress of grief we can be quick to anger, and that anger can shift swiftly to a guilt that can further injure us. It may be hard to find perspective at these times, but I found that just going through the act of forgiving myself for my extreme mood swings helped me find balance. I believe that being gentle to myself, and looking for forgiveness, reduced the impact of these raw emotions on my health and mental state.

My hard won balance let me see my son's life in a new light, and I gained a deeper understanding of the kind of a man he was. Most of all, I gained a renewed certainty of his love for me. Perspective can be so hard to find when grieving, but so precious when found.

The Check

I hold the check in limp fingers, feeling nothing
No excitement, no anticipation
just dust: in my mouth, and in my soul

Wergild for the death of my son

Early in my grief I thought he left still angry
left naming no beneficiary
How could he forget us, forget me?

Despairing, not for loss of money, but afraid I lost his love

Burning in shameful envy of those he may have loved more
selfishly yearning for his attention, his care

Later, as I sifted the remains of his life
sorting out letters filled with pleas for payment
warnings from creditors, threats to ruin his reputation

piles of bills unopened, ignored

I was struck by his casual disregard
for the petty aspects of life
the day-to-day detritus

Contrast this with his magnificent impact on the lives he touched
myriad lives changed by knowing him
working with him, loving him

His focus *was* true

Obsessed by a passion to teach, share knowledge, give wisdom
to use all his moments helping others learn
to believe in the power within them

and see how truly important they are to this world

To understand the tremendous value of their worth
accept their duty to share unique and precious gifts
as he did with such love and gentle care

He was consumed
driven by an unquenchable desire
to make everyone he touched

understand their true place in life
to see the divine within
and unlock their hidden gifts

He did not neglect me. He did not forget us
He was just busy changing the world
one mind at a time

He loved me too

~

Chapter Eight

Here there be Dragons

embrace your shadow
learn from what you would deny
gifts hide in the dark

IN EVERY LANDSCAPE YOU WILL find dangerous places, filled with strange twists and unfinished business. Welcome to the dark side of my soul where my shadow self lives. I would often visit here during my periods of introspection to examine my memories of events that tied me to the past. I would look at buried wounds that had never healed and the losses of a stunted childhood that I had never properly grieved.

I see my dark side as a cave, guarded by powerful dragons, containing a deep well of smothered feelings, hidden desires and unfulfilled potential. This is where I buried the parts of myself I was ashamed of, the shadowed elements of my being I had to deny and keep from view. I hid them so deep that even I could not see them, and forgot they existed. Those abandoned parts of me cried out to be realized, constantly clamoring for my attention. I would not allow their voices to be heard for many years, so I suffered inside—unheard, unrealized.

The sorrow of grief led me to reexamine my life. I discovered that there were many parts of my personality buried inside, they were the parts of me I couldn't accept. Unfortunately, when I buried them I also hid away many good parts of my psyche that I needed to grow into a complete person. It was like applying an emergency tourniquet to stop bleeding. I fixed the immediate problem, but I also damaged myself.

The problem with hiding problems instead of solving them is they never go away. You just give them time to grow teeth so they can bite you deeper when they eventually do return. Your subconscious self will find a way to force you to deal with these hidden parts and problems, even to the point of sabotaging your relationships, self image and health.

That sabotage was the reason I could never find peace and happiness in my life. I hid too many vital parts of myself at an early age so I never developed properly. I could only see myself in a warped and cloudy mirror.

I thought I was ugly, unwanted, stupid, cowardly, and hateful. I was a sinner who drove away my father. A worthless, twisted thing unworthy of love. A failure. A fool. I was a bad and dirty little boy, who learned to expect nothing so I wouldn't be disappointed when I got nothing.

Those buried parts of me had to be found and reclaimed if I was ever to be whole. They were hidden in my shadow. As I said earlier, this inner work of confronting and accepting my shadow self, was vital to making me a complete person armed with the power and strength of my true self. The dark side is where I found the armor and sword I needed to become a soul warrior, it is also where I fought some of my best battles.

I learned of the dark side and my shadow self in conversations with my first therapist, Gail. She was originally just helping me cope with my grief, but she soon saw deeper troubles in me. She once paid me a wonderful complement by calling me a Mensch, which is Yiddish for a person of integrity and honor. She told me that she had never met anyone who ate so much pain for other people so they wouldn't have to taste it.

I also consulted an excellent hypnotherapist, Sheri. She recommend I read Debbie Ford's book, *The Dark Side of the Light Chasers*, to learn more about what the dark side was and how to approach it. Debbie Ford also wrote *The Shadow Effect*, along with Deepak Chopra and Marianne Williamson, that goes in more detail about the origin and mechanisms of the dark side. This is a good guide to self exploration of your shadow self. It taught me that when we bury the parts of our self that we feel must be denied, great gifts are often buried with them.

I learned that when guilt prompts me to examine my actions, I must be gentle with myself and forgive the action if no harm was done. I then look inside for parts of my psyche I formally denied and embrace that abandoned part of myself. I try to understand how that lost element that could make me more complete. I then look further to see if there are hidden gifts I can reclaim.

To illustrate how this works, I was confronted by an angry woman who tried to provoke me into fight with her. She used extreme measures to prompt a rise in me, and at one point I actually wanted to hit her. Of course I didn't act on that impulse, that is just something I could not do. I felt terrible afterward and used the dark side techniques to work with my feelings. I forgave myself for that impulsive desire, and looked deep to figure out why I reacted so strongly. I recalled an event that happened when my mother told my father she wanted a divorce and asked him to leave the house. I was eight years old, my sister Jeannine was six, and my brother Don was four.

The next night my father pounded on the door demanding to be let in. She refused and he kicked in the door. All of us kids were sitting terrified on the couch in the front room and watched while he beat her. I was powerless to move and protect her. I felt like a little coward. I was horrified and afraid I would grow up just like my father. I never wanted to hurt a woman, so I took those thoughts of male aggression against women and buried them deep in my dark side. What I didn't know was that I also buried a lot of my male power at the same time. As a result, I was unable to bring my essential male power into my relationships.

I grew into a passive male in a powerful body. My mother would reinforce my passivity by systematically crushing any aggression my brother or I showed, asking us if we wanted to be like our father. I became afraid of hurting women with any sort of aggression. In spite of all the safeguards I set up, at times my anger would still slip out. I would then be mortified and turned my anger against myself, as I was taught to do. I didn't know that my missing power jeopardized my professional and personal relationships. I couldn't access my passion, because it's source was locked away in my shadow self.

I remembered the night terrors that haunted my dreams soon after my father left for good. My strongest nightmare centered on a black maned lion who lived in my back yard. I was afraid he would devour me, but some part of me wanted to be eaten by that beast. I could never reconcile my mixed emotions of repulsion and attraction. My therapist told me this was a dream of abandonment. I examined my nightmare and reasoned I was feeling regret at burying my power and wanted to be reunited with it.

I went into a meditative state to fully visualize my dreaded lion. I defied my childhood terror and opened myself fully to my beast. I felt him bounding across a vast plain to come to me, and I welcomed him in with fierce joy. My feelings of completeness and power were exhilarating. This was my first encounter with the greatest gift I found in my shadow self, my hidden beast. I now channel this immense power and passion into my relationships and my art; but then, shouldn't any good relationship be art?

I discovered we all ride a beast that is our original nature, subjugated and contained deep within us. To catch a glimpse of the beast try arguing with any two year old. I hid my beast out of fear and false shame. I found when I reclaimed and used these gifts I had the freedom to use them with love instead of anger. I was not my father.

At that time, I was in a new relationship with a woman I adored, but she said that my passion was missing from our relationship. My strong male energy now burned brightly inside of me.

The next time we met I walked silently to her. I pressed my entire body against hers, trapping her against the wall and kissed her deeply. She stepped back, looked at me with eyes wide open in delight and said, "Now *that's* what I'm talking about!"

My beast happily growled agreement with a deep rumbling purr.

I speak here only of my male beast; that's what I know from experience. However, I have also learned to know my partner's female beast. She is magnificently equal to mine in independence, power and passion. When we join to celebrate our dualities, we seem to exist in a strong attractive field where magic occurs.

My essential male power helps me step up in my relationship when my partner needs me to. I step up to defend, protect, comfort, console, praise, listen, but most of all, to be the man my lover needs me to be. To be always the best man I can be, first for myself and then for her.

I learned to step up because it's the right and honorable thing to do, even when it's not easy or convenient. These actions show clearly my honor and respect for both of us, and for the love we share. The more I practiced this selfless act, the more I built a reciprocal trust with my partner that formed a strong foundation for love and true intimacy.

Healthy male passion was also necessary for me to successfully participate in this fulfilling and powerful relationship. Our passion opened both of us to soaring joy. I became the real man I was always meant to be. If I hadn't have changed; we wouldn't have been.

My poems in this chapter explain the sources of my early injuries and misconceptions. These poems tell of who I was but no longer am. Here are the darkside fears and dragons I confronted, accepted, and pulled into my heart. These poems helped me find the missing and neglected parts of myself that I needed to own to be whole.

I brought my dark side into the light and found my hidden gifts.

In my fractured childhood, I learned many false lessons and believed many untruths. I thought I sacrificed my childhood, at the age of eight, trying to be the man of the house. I took on the duty to protect my little sister and brother, only to fail at everything I did to help them.

I felt this was my original failure, much like the original sin the nuns told me about. This failure set the pattern for so many years to come. It was only when I saw my eight year old grandson playing with his classmates, that I realized I would never have expected any of them to take on the burdens I accepted at that tender age. I knew then I had judged myself too harshly.

All those years ago, my anger at the drunken red rages of my father caused me to wish him gone. My devil granted my wish, and my father left. I believed my parents divorced because of me. That was the secret sin I spent almost five decades of my life repenting.

I saw myself as worthless and unlovable, but I reasoned that I could, perhaps, be useful. I learned to serve. I learned to be useful so others would want me. I learned to protect so others would accept me. I lived to be used, if not to be happy. I was blind to my true nature and my true worth. I didn't know how to love myself. If I couldn't love me, what love did I have to share with another?

These poems capture the broken parts of me that needed to be healed before I could find happiness in my changed life. Some of these parts I wanted to deny but needed desperately to understand and accept. I found many hidden treasures here guarded by powerful dragons.

Rather than try to slay these guardians, I learned to accept them, absorb their power, and render them harmless with my love.

I didn't understand that I created these dragons to protect me from seeing who I truly was. I thought if anyone really knew me they would run from me in horror. In time, I learned that my true self is more wonderful than I ever could have imagined. This is my truth. This is your truth. Know it and act on it.

Bonsai Soul at Sorrows Edge

Grief forced me to examine all my losses, including my lost childhood. *Bonsai Soul at Sorrows Edge* recreates how it felt to be a throwaway kid with a sharp intellect. I saw so much but could not see myself. I was always afraid, and could not free myself from the endless cycle of self doubt, self pity, and self condemnation.

Bonsai Soul at Sorrows Edge

I dwelt alone in the darkling of the pale

An ocean of sorrow held within
My bonsai soul twisted to escape
the awful weight of their eyes upon my skin

Spawned by fire, born of ice
Psyche slashed by chilling knives of love denied
powerless to hinder Fear's full reign

Innocence vanished in the howling winds of burning rage

Swimming the shallows over jagged rocks
slipping unseen through murky currents
walking the shore amongst the wrack of the tide

I shied from the depths

afraid to go too deep; lest
swallowed by the pain
I forget somehow to breathe

It took the deaths to drive me to the depths
Death of mother, death of son, death of hope
they drove me deep to sorrows core

past shimmering limits of all safeguards

To the unlighted realm of oblivion
the chilling eye of chaos' storm
to the depths I knew would hold me fast

in an unremitting embrace, I fled

Reality shrunk into that singular spot
that tiny stain in space
all hope abandoned

Forlorn, I shivered in the moment
of the midnight of my soul
Staggered by the knowledge of how much was lost

I gibbered at the dark

I knew that pain
that aching throb
when tears at last were gone

All emotion gone to sorrow
driven out by the awful weight of grief
I wait for breath

I dwelt alone in the darkling of the pale

FATHER

Father is my memory of being a frightened child of six, hiding behind the kitchen door as my father raged through the house destroying everything in an alcohol fueled rage. I was holding onto a bag of tiny powdered sugar donuts that I didn't want him to throw into the bonfire he built in the backyard. These were mine.

Also hidden in that little space, was my younger sister Jeannine. She was my constant shadow, and I her protector. I can still feel her tiny fists shaking in fear, pressed tight to the small of my back, as I shielded her. Even at that age, I knew to put myself between her and harm.

I don't remember my father's face, but I remember his bloody hands.

My mother used to be *my* protector, who would hug me and tell me I was good. She would tell me stories about the pixies and fairies who lived in the backyard. That was the safe place where I played, and they were the invisible playmates I loved.

That night my mother put on an icy cold face that never left her. I don't remember any more hugs or stories. There was no one left to tell me I was good. I felt abandoned by her, and that abandonment continued until I left home at seventeen. That night there no more safe places in my life. I screamed in silence from my hiding place, watching all the pixies burn.

Father

I remember a laughing god who held me squealing
high over his head while I held on tight
to his black curly hair

I remember a gentle dark haired goddess
who told me stories of pixies and fairies
living in our back yard

vanished one day

what cruel god took those loving, caring people
replacing them with my parents?

to love father showed disloyalty to mother

sandpaper face, fleshy and scarred
sweet warm alcohol breath fumed by cheap brandy

slurred words, snakelike weaving walk
pale blue eyes unfocused, red and streaming

skirting the line between rage and self pity
violence and sorrow

a wandering litany of grievance and grudge
flaring at a slight to a bonfires roar

consuming all within his grasp
tender lives clutched in bloodied hands

i hide in the space behind the kitchen door
swallowing terror

flames dancing beyond my tears
i watch while all the pixies burn

exciting to a boy caught in the windstorm
that took away his childhood

~

I could not count on the support of my parents so I created a shadowy protector to watch over me when I was scared or in danger. I was often afraid and very lonely. I never actually saw my protector, but I could feel him close to me when my fear was the strongest. During my time of transformation, Sheri used hypnotherapy to help me get past some of the buried safeguards I built when I walled off parts of my shadow self.

I had always been able to let my mind drift and direct my attention into self guided meditation, so Sheri found me a willing patient. She would put me into a trance state and lead me into my dark side on focused trips of exploration. One time she asked me to search for my inner child. I found myself at eight, sitting on a bare wooden floor, crying alone in a dark and empty room. I spoke to my little child and told him everything would be okay. I would always be close by when he needed me. I had the strange feeling that I somehow became that shadowy protector I dreamt about when I was that scared little child. Holding myself in that vision was perhaps when I started loving myself.

Little Whip

I suffered through Catholic school, punished regularly by the Good Sisters for my inability to conform to their rules and philosophies. The nuns and I were never on good terms. I suppose that I started it on the first day of Catholic school. I began my time at St. Marks School in the third grade, soon after my mother divorced my father. He didn't allow religion in the house, so now my mother could start taking us to church. I was a little pagan in a strange land who found everything about this new world a bit silly.

I had never seen a nun before and couldn't quite make out what they were. They dressed in long black skirts that brushed the ground as they glided around the classroom. I wondered if they were wearing roller skates. I lifted the hem of one of the black habits and found out fast how upset they could get with "nasty little boys".

That's when I found out they could hurt us any time they wanted, for as long as they wanted. They kept doing just that for my endless string of transgressions. No one would dare to stop them, certainly not my mother. School became another place of pain.

The worst thing they did was to try to force me to fear God. I never understood why I was required to fear him if he was the one who created me. They were quite clear about that in the Catechism Lessons.

Q: WHO MADE US?

A: GOD MADE US.

Q: WHY DID GOD MAKE US?

A: GOD MADE US TO SHOW FORTH HIS GOODNESS AND TO SHARE WITH US HIS EVERLASTING HAPPINESS IN HEAVEN.

Q: WHAT MUST WE DO TO GAIN THE HAPPINESS OF HEAVEN?

A: TO GAIN THE HAPPINESS OF HEAVEN WE MUST KNOW, LOVE, AND SERVE GOD IN THIS WORLD.

I found nothing about fear in my much thumbed Baltimore Catechism, but when I tried to point this out to the Good Sisters they got very upset with me again. More pain.

Children often draw extreme conclusions from incomplete information, especially when it is presented by a seemingly absolute authority. I learned the penalties for failing to obey every direct command from that authority, but I could never let go of my doubts. I discovered that outward acts of obedience could fool them into thinking I was submitting. I never yielded my complete obedience to them. I would always fight them. I was stubborn and smart, but I had no tactical sense.

Eventually, through many applications of painful correction, I learned deep guilt and shame from those women. I applied this new knowledge to my understanding of the world and solidified my belief that I failed to measure up to my responsibilities. I did the nuns one better and started punishing myself for my perceived sins. I learned how to wield my *Little Whip*. I became a child flagellanti in an attempt to, "mortify my flesh and redeem my soul." I wanted to live like the Saints. I didn't want to burn in Hell for eternity, and I figured this was what I had to do to prevent that from happening.

Sometimes I would start bleeding in class from my self-inflicted punishments, and my classmates would scream and run away. *Little Whip* captures some of the self punishing trap I fell into. The nuns could only punish me for brief moments and pain faded quickly; I could do a much better job of it. I eventually passed beyond the need for outward expression and internalized my punishments.

During that time, I buried many parts of myself that couldn't be forced into the rigid Catholic mold, as taught by the nuns. It took me decades to reclaim those lost parts. Eventually, I outgrew my attempts to obey at the cost of being labeled a pariah. I stood outside the pale, just within a stone's throw.

I did win one victory against the nuns. In the eighth grade we were given an assignment to write an essay about the sacrament of Communion. I turned in a scholarly paper, with footnotes, titled, *Ritual Cannibalism in the Catholic Church, Eating God*. The penguins went berserk and sent me to the Monsignor for punishment.

I found myself standing at rigid attention in front of his desk while he read my paper. I had no idea what he was going to do to me, and my mind was racing with wild acts of retribution at his hand. The nuns couldn't break me, but he was more powerful. He ran the Church. There was a glare on his glasses, so I couldn't see his eyes. I imagined flames in them. Maybe he could send me straight to Hell. He made several strange noises as he read, and my feet got really itchy from sweat. I wanted to run but was frozen to the spot. Perhaps this was my stubborn defiance asserting itself in the midst of my terror.

I forgot how to breathe.

He softly put the paper down and stared at me for a minute. Finally he smiled and said the paper was well written, but I really should not play tricks on the nuns. It wasn't very nice, and I would always lose. He made me promise to never do it again and to not tell the nuns that he hadn't punished me. He gave me a little punch on the shoulder, shook his finger at me, and told me to go home. He was my new hero, and I wanted to become a priest. I outgrew that too.

Little Whip

The whip burns just for the moment
but moments pass
Hot blossoms of pain cannot long endure

What remain eternal are the whip
and the intent
if you are the wielder

Alchemy of Care

Later in life I found a classmate who was a silent witness to the pain, and systematic abandonment, of my childhood. It helped me to know that someone had seen my pain and cared for me. This knowledge helped me come to terms with my buried grief for the loss of love and safety in my life, all those years ago.

I could finally morn that loss, and heal those old wounds. I started to believe that I really could be loved, and found some comfort in her arms. Soon after this healing, I started my search for the one who would love me for who I was, not just for what I could give.

Alchemy of Care is my poem of thanks to that silent childhood witness.

Alchemy of Care

You saw my pain and saved those visions
tucked lovingly away in a tender heart
Sharp shards of sorrow enfolded in gentle softness

slowly transmuting in the alchemy of your care

Desolate I grew, stunted in spirit.
Incomplete, alien, isolated
judged too inferior to be human

cast out to struggle alone beyond the pale

Childhood snatched from little fingers
by a cold and unforgiving world

Unknown to me you cared when I was lost and lonely
You return to me now
the forgotten fragments of my youth

held safe these years, in trust for my return

Your witness of my aching past, thrown open to me now
Releasing keys to free that fettered child
to open dark and hidden hurt, and salve the ancient wounds

perhaps to remake me all anew

To close the cracks that grew to chasms
ease the aches that bloomed to sadness
replace rejection with awakened love

To regain my lost and scattered self
abraded bits torn from a tender core

I grasp these precious elements
fragrant with your essence
lost, missing for so long

My soul draws them deep inside
filling the voids
those empty places with your grace

Restored, I turn to embrace you
with strong and grateful arms

~

Dust

This is the first poem I ever wrote. It contains my first acceptance of the ephemeral nature of my life as I prepared myself for war. I wrote *Dust* in 1968 when I was in the Navy, standing watch over a landscape of sand dunes. I was 19 years old, far from home, feeling homesick and very alone.

I was an avid science fiction reader and felt inspired to write my first poem as if my watch was on a distant planet that hungered for my life. This landscape was strange and alien to me, so I let my mind drift and wrote what I felt. I knew I should have been more vigilant, but I figured the sand dunes weren't going to kill me, were they?

Dust

The wind slides across the pavement
sending puffs of dust to wash my boots with slippery dryness

The sun retreats letting the cold take me
my thin shirt offers little opposition

I stand immobilized by a stark landscape
the touch of loneliness at my throat

My lungs pull in a bit of air
dry and laced with alien scents

that drew my moisture like a leech
to replace it with a coat of grit

The wind buffets my face and whips my hair over one eye
as if to hide the creeping dune of silt

I watch her as she flows smoothly forward
to bring exquisite symmetry to the tumbled brick

She wraps my foot in her softness
and sends a tendril of herself through my laces

filling my boot
with warmth stolen from the sun

Like a lover she caresses and strokes my entire frame
And when I open my mouth to thank her for her care

with infinite softness she hushes me
filling my mouth with her kiss

As I slowly sink into her arms
I remember the ancient words

"Dust thou art and unto dust thou shalt return"

Chapter Nine

Poems of Happiness

know that in pain's depths
blades of grass split rocks in two
joy will shatter grief

Grieving is not always unremitting sadness. George Bonnano made this observation in his book, *The Other Side of Sadness*, "... bereaved people are able to have genuinely pleasurable experiences, to laugh or indulge in moments of joy, even in the earliest days and weeks after loss." I found that there are times in the midst of grief when we can feel tenderness, appreciate beauty, and see the humor in a situation.

As inappropriate as it sounds, just a few days after my loss I found comfort in a brief moment of humor. I was sitting in the funeral home, just two days after Aaron's death, signing the paperwork for his burial. As I wrote the date on the form, it struck me like a slap in my face that it was my birthday.

I started to slide into another grief driven meltdown, when the door to the office flew open, and in walked a young man dressed in a Los

Angeles SWAT uniform, complete with helmet and assault rifle. We all sat transfixed by this dark apparition, then I recognized him as one of my son's De Molay brothers. He heard the news of Aaron's death that morning and heard we were at the cemetery. He was working on a protection detail at the airport, and had a fellow officer fill in for him so he could rush over to give his support. He ran over to me and Lisa, pulling us into his arms.

I couldn't help but laugh at this surreal situation, and at the astonishment on the face of the undertaker. For that moment I felt only comfort and gratitude at the devotion of this wonderful young man, and a bit of joy flashed through me. Sadness and pain was held at bay for a little while. Grief seems to be not a set series of stages but a complex mixture of the several attributes of grief that differ from moment to moment for each of us, in composition, intensity and duration.

Madison's Eyes

Sometime later, I was in a rather difficult phase of the grieving process and shared my poems with a friend, the only poet I knew. I wasn't really sure if what I was writing was worth reading. He said he wished he could tap into that same, rich vein. He encouraged me to continue while the muse was active and challenged me to write something lighter. He told me to simply think of one of my happiest moments and see where it took me. I immediately thought of the birth of my oldest granddaughter, Madison. I felt the joy of that moment and, to my surprise, the poem flowed out of me.

Madison's Eyes captures the first moment I saw her, just minutes after her birth. I held her in my arms, she opened her eyes for the first time, and I was forever hers.

When she was just a few years older, Madison grew into a delightful and peaceful little lady, eyes filled with wisdom beyond her years. Madison has a quick and facile mind. From an early age, she and I would play 'mind games' where we would imagine up a room filled with white winged butterflies and then describe how we painted them with our invisible paint brushes.

We would envision an enormous ball floating in the room before us, make it spin with our minds until it was just a blur in space and then STOP IT, and send it spinning in the other direction. So much fun, and what a beauty she has become!

Madison's Eyes

She opens her eyes for the first time
and I fall into them

Unfocused, so quiet, so intense

Drinking in the first sights
of her infant life

writing first memories
on a clean slate

she stares so intently into my eyes

I feel the new mind behind them
studying my face

fixing my features for all time

Eyes locked in sweet embrace
a little hand wraps softly around my heart

She owns me
She will always be my sweetheart
She still is

~

Little Dragon

The next poem was about my grandson Brandon, who is known variously as; Little Dragon, Sugarbowl, and Big Boy Brandon. *Little Dragon* is an attempt to catch him at age three (a tough job). Brandon attacks life head on with the playful fierce gaze of a dragon blazing from his eyes.

He is now a powerful young man, both physically and mentally, with a gentle heart and a strong sense of justice. He will always protect those who are smaller and weaker than he is.

I saw clearly the difference between my first two grandchildren when my mother first met Brandon. She watched his playful exuberance for a while with a smile filled with whimsy and wistful remembrance.

She then patted my daughters hand to comfort her whispering, "It skipped a generation Dear."

Little Dragon

Big boy Brandon walks with a swagger
sugar bowl arms pumping back and forth
Three years old, master of the universe!

Favorite word: No
Favorite cry: NEVER

Filled to the top with courage
fearing nothing, loving everyone
except Barbie

he does not like Barbie
SHE is a girls toy
she belongs to Sister

But he *loves* Dragons
He feeds them treats
usually Barbie

Boundless energy, brimming with excitement
a powerhouse of playfulness
exploding with giggles at the slightest tickle

He scales the mighty chair to its lofty peak
dives off head first, roaring and breathing fire
onto his daddy

He jumps up a Jedi, spinning and kicking the air
A high pitched "hee ya" bursts from his lips
scaring off evildoers and poody heads

Splashing in the tub, swimming in the ocean
spinning in a whirlpool
piling masses of soapsuds on his indulgent sister

he douses her clean with a loaded bath toy

He bursts forth spraying water
wraps up in his fluffy towel
gallops screaming from the room

transformed in a flash into a ten foot baby blue monster
into Spirit the defiant stallion, into the lion king
into a naked hopping frog

Bare feet flying down the hallway
bare bottom wiggling as he runs still wet from the tub
he casts off the towel, beats his tiny chest with a Tarzan yell

Alpha male personified

Sturdy body scrubbed clean and ready for bed, after a story
and a drink, and a hug
another story?

He slips into sleep, crafting visions, flying with dragons
Quiet returns to the house
a bit of stillness for a while

until little dragon awakes

~

UNEXPECTED ANGEL

Grayson, my youngest granddaughter, is our *Unexpected Angel.* She was born five and a half years after her big brother Brandon, and she is the delight of the family. Grayson, Baby Gray to Mommy, combines Madison's wit, beauty and grace with Brandon's strength, determination and humor. She is quite a handful.

Everyone indulges her bright sense of humor and her frilly, girly-girl manner. She is convinced she was born a princess and we must cater to her every whim. Brandon is fiercely protective of her and will sometimes carry her around, while she squirms in his arms and slugs him. She often makes big brother the butt of her jokes, but she loves him back with the same ferocity.

Grayson worships her big sister, and became the mascot of Madison's gymnastic exhibition team when she turned three. She had the same uniform as the big girls and would solemnly march out in the middle of a formal competition, do a forward summersault, then strike and hold the classic, arms out, arched back, gymnastic pose. The audience would go wild. She is now a full member of her own show team and never forgets to strike that same dramatic pose. Grayson always flings herself into my arms as soon as she sees me, wrapping me up in a loving hug. She graciously lets me call her Baby, even though she is now a grown up princess of five.

Unexpected Angel

Mommy thought she was finally done
with all the joys of birth

She only had to feel your smile
embrace her in a dream

A shining princess you were born
a princess you shall ever be

Noblesse Oblige in tiny form
in spite of all the giggling

You came to us all wrapped in pink
and pink remains your hue

You always choose to wear a skirt
"PrinCess does Not wear Pants"

You bend our language to your will
words spring from your rosebud lips

Banana Slugs are naked snails
butterflies are futterflies

We laugh at every little joke
you didn't know you made

Innocence shining boldly forth
from soft and melting eyes

Strawbebbies smeared on clean pink blouse
choclick milk adorns your face

"Who made this mess?" your mommy cries
"Not me! I didn't didit!"

A thousand kittens playfulness
the grace of every futterfly

our unexpected angel girl
with the heart of a Samurai!

You don big Brothers football gear
smear mascara on your cheeks

jump screaming on him focusing
on a tiny movie screen

"Mommy mommy listen to me
Brother saida big BAD WORD!"

You snatch big Sisters new cell phone
while she watches her TV show

eyes squinting tight with sharp intent
thumbs darting fast on every key

dispannobu johee hublee
flies through the web to tickle me

You asked me if I'd stay for good
I pledged to do my best

to come back every day I could
and miss you all the rest

Hey, hey my little Baby Gray
how many hearts did you touch today?

You can start your list with mine

~

Sitting with a Seagull

The morning following my dark night of the soul, I found some time to sit on that balcony and absorb the peace of the day. A suspicious seagull landed on the railing and kept watching me. I had no food for him, so I expected him to leave.

He sat with me for a long time, and I felt comfort in the independence of his company. I wanted to capture the moment, so I would never forget it.

I painted a word picture of the experience in *Sitting with a Seagull.*

Sitting with a Seagull

I sit on a rustic sun bleached chair
perched on a balcony in early morning light

enjoying a fresh cold breeze, spiced with salt
as it flowed across my face

Thin white clouds on light blue sky
cream into a soft lavender mist

smeared across the horizon
Patches of dark kelp float on a silvery aquamarine sea

Tiny seabirds skim the surface
searching out careless fish

Undulating waves seek the shore
break for a moment in explosions of white froth

on dark rocks sprinkled about the bay
then hurry on

to crash against cracked and fissured rocks
jagged, and fringed with pine

Deep green needles float on sentry trunks of weathered wood

rooted in red rich loam

A dark froth of leaves mimic the ocean spray

Squadrons of orange butterflies
wings warmed by the waxing sun

rise up to greet the day

A seagull drops to the railing beside me
cool and splendid in white and gray

wearing a red dot, like a spot of blood
on pale ivory beak

Ebony eyes watching for a morsel of food
for a move of menace

We sit together, thinking private thoughts in silent contemplation
Sharing solitude

Peace

~

Searchers

When I wrote *Searchers* in early 2004, NASA had just sent two robot explorers to rove the surface of Mars. The primary goal of this mission was to search for evidence that Mars once held sufficient water, and atmosphere, to support life.

Several theories suggested how a water rich atmosphere could have been lost. One was that the immense gravity well of Jupiter pulled the atmosphere into space.

Another theory was that a wayward planet passed through our solar system and flew so close to Mars that it changed the planet's orbit to one farther from the warmth of our sun. The molten core of Mars grew cold and hard, so the magnetic field that held in the atmosphere grew too weak to prevent the solar wind from stripping the precious air of Mars into the dead of space.

What struck me most about the mission, was the tenuous thread of data that connected the searchers on Mars to the observers on Earth. Was this like the thread of memory that still connected me to my lost son? I tried to capture the hunger, and yearning, I felt for the answer to this question. Is there life out there in that place I cannot go?

Searchers

Insectile explorers crawl through frigid Martian valleys
rolling gingerly over rusty litter

Grinding rock, sifting sand
blazing a path with shifting lights
to search out erosion

Sipping alien air, sampling for elusive, essential volatiles
Looking for signs water's womb once pooled here
pulsing with ancient life

Data streams upward from twitching flat antennae
screaming millions of miles to reach the waiting throng

huddled tight before glowing screens
intently poised
transfixed by naked desire

Slaking somewhat their deep, intense thirst for knowledge

Did water once flow on this alien plain?
Did rivers carve these valleys?
Washing these very rocks, seeping deep into this ruddy sand?

In a wetter, warmer time, did this planet once birth life?

Did the grave mass of Jupiter suck vital essence from this soil?
Rip water from thinning atmosphere
desiccate vast areas of a once fertile land?

Steal the liquid riches of this place?

Or, was it the very motion of a suicide world
hurtling through space?

Did erratic orbits plunge this rock
into long, bleak winters of loss?

Feeble gravity unable to halt
enormous out gassings of its vital elements
all life plucked out by the aching chill of space

Is our appetite for answers driven by the hunger of our loneliness?

Are we alone in the depths?
Are we the sum of thinking life?

Does another intelligence, in some other place
vast distances from here
also ponder a darkling sky for meaning?

We grasp at hope and cast out our net

Trying to be Beat in the 21st Century

I was reading the *Holy Barbarians* by Lawrence Lipton, and was inspired to write my own rant. He chronicled the Beat movement in Venice, California, while it was still in progress. The movement was focused on two coffee houses on the Venice Beach: the Venice West, and the Gas House.

I grew up watching the Beats hanging around the Gas House, but I was too young to be allowed in. I was attracted to their intensity and freedom. They were the parents, and odd relatives, of my friends at school. The Beats didn't feel obligated to follow any of the normal conventions of society.

They seemed to hear a different song than the rest of us, and I strained to hear it too. Mr. Lipton brought all that yearning back to me, and I started wondering what it is to be Beat today. Out screamed *Trying to be Beat in the 21st Century.*

I remember writing the first few lines as I was falling asleep. I kept waking up and adding thoughts to it on my iPhone notepad. When I was done, I sent it out to some friends. Just for kicks, dig? They really liked it, but one of them said it was a strong political statement. That surprised me, because I meant it all in fun.

The more I looked at the poem, the more I agreed. I think I tapped into those lessons I learned in front of the Gas House from my Beatnik teachers. Now I have to walk the walk. Do you feel the need to walk it too? Maybe just a little? Be careful, freedom is intoxicating. It's easy to get hooked, but Man what a Ride!

Trying to be Beat in the 21st Century

Where the MilitaryIndustrialComplex has given birth to the Web
that unites us all with liberty and freedom of expression
that makes China cringe

Where we look at Modern Art with Nostalgia
and Kerouac On the Road
gathers dust on the shelf of a thrift store

Where the Hepcats and Hepkittens
have gray hair, and grandchildren
who wonder at jazz trapped in vinyl

and how we ever lived
without games in our phones
in our pockets <snap>

Where I tap my rant on my own phone
with an apple on the back
and the Whole World that I keep in my pocket <zap>

Where the Venice West is a Starbucks
wherein a Rasta Barista makes decaf Frappachinos
with white chocolate raspberry hempmilk

for tattooed code monkeys
who dream digital dreams
of android sheep <pow>

Where Bird still blows his horse fueled chops
in the valley nights, whispering notes of rebellion
in the young ears of sleeping suburban children

Where the seeds of the Beat still move
in the hearts of those chosen few
who see beyond the hype on the tube

and fly above
the interwoven lies of the net
to seek the truth

The Truth Hepcats and Hepkittens

The only response, the only defense
to the crushing power of media-ocrity
is the single boldest act of defiance

the pure sweet act of creation

Blow my Babies, blow Truth into being
<SNAP>

~

Now ~ Between Memory and Imagination

C.S. Lewis wrote *A Grief Observed* to capture his experiences with grief. In it he wondered what became of his wife after she died. If she still was — *where* was she? Sorrow prompts us to look inward and deal with the weighty questions of death.

I found myself, lost at times, pondering where my son went and what kind of existence he was experiencing other than the one in my imagination.

I often meditate on the moment in time we live in, suspended between the twin illusions of memory and imagination, when we invoke images from our past and future. Lewis was struggling with what 'now' means, and the nature of his wife's existence, when he wrote, "If the dead are not in time, or not in our sort of time, is there any clear difference, when we speak of them, between was and is and will be?"

Our language gets a bit tangled when we wrestle with the differences between our awareness of our present experience in the now, and our visualization of moments from our past and our future. I tried to express this difficulty in my poem *Now ~ Between Memory and Imagination.*

We can make those illusionary moments become real for us, so we feel like we are actually living in them and sharing them with our lost ones. These experiences become so real that it's hard to realize they are only illusions. Sometimes the line between illusion and experience becomes blurred when we are grieving, so we can create those precious visitations where we share moments with our beloved.

The difference between what is real, and what is fantasy, pales in comparison to the comfort and solace we can draw from those moments. It is important to keep our sense of wonder and not take ourselves too seriously at these times. We need to be gentle with ourselves and keep these loving connections alive.

Now ~ Between Memory and Imagination

Consider the difference
between that what Was, and
that what Is Now, and then that what Will Be

I am who I Was, I am who I Am
and I am who Will Be
when my Then, then appears

What I view as my Self
is continual flux
shifting now, as my eyes try to see me

Feel the vibrations that ring when I sing
who I Am when between
all the times that I am

Now I find I must ask
who I Am when I am
When I'm *THERE*

is there any **There** there?

RhymeTime

I was presenting some of my work at an poetry reading and was asked why my poems didn't rhyme. I found myself getting angry and sat down to write *RhymeTime* in a fit of pique. I then wondered why I had this reaction. I remembered that I started writing poetry in the late sixties, but stopped when I was in Viet-Nam.

When I returned home, I quickly realized that digging ditches was not going to provide much security for my wife and the twins. I started working on my engineering degrees and events overtook me.

When I finally felt it was time to write, I took my work to an English teacher at a local University to get an opinion of it's worth. I was told that whatever I was writing, it didn't rhyme, so it wasn't poetry. I got so upset by this that I threw all of my work away and forgot about writing poetry.

When I started the grief process, I found solace in writing poetry. I found that grief took up so much of my attention that I was freed from any self criticism. As a result, I wrote freely and with abandon. This taught me to trust my first draft and to avoid critical thinking while creating. The creative side of my brain is a much better writer than the critical side of my brain. I know that *RhymeTime* is a bit silly, but sometimes a little silliness is just what we need.

RhymeTime

I simply haven't time to rhyme
I strive instead, within my head
to find that match, that certain catch
the word that makes the BEAT complete

If phrasings' apt, my reader's trapped
Attention caught, to view my thought
pulled in to find, my piece of mind
in syncopated beat that's reet

Chapter Ten

Poems of Love

10

lips brush in the night
whispered love from soul to soul
lingers on my tongue

Now we enter a different part of the soul's landscape, one filled with verdant glades and secret grottos. Part of my transformation was a deep examination of what I needed in my life to be happy. I spent some time getting used to the newly integrated parts of myself that I rescued from the dark side. I learned how to honor and love myself. Self love was a breakthrough for me. I then realized that I could actually be happy in my changed life, so I took out a fresh sheet of paper and wrote what I needed to be happy.

First need. I need to share love with my Creator. I came to an elegant, yet simple, view of Heaven and Hell from conversations with a Jesuit. Perhaps this is faithful to his view, perhaps it is only my interpretation. The conversation took place decades ago but the ideas lingered.

We were all created as an act of love. Our Creator only wants us to return that love fully. At the moment of our death, we enter a timeless moment of eternity where we are given the choice to return, or not return, that love. If we choose to return love, we enter into the state of heaven. If for some reason we are unable to return love, knowing that love is freely offered to us, we exist in the state of hell. That is all that matters.

All other theological philosophy, no matter what religious belief system it springs from, seems to pale in comparison for me. When I meditate on this timeless moment, I move into a state of reverie and refreshment.

In effect, the timeless states of heaven and hell are merely our act of creating, or not creating, a bond of unconditional love with our Creator at the moment of our death. This is our assurance that what was created with love will never be abandoned.

Second need. I need to love myself, accepting all parts of myself equally and without reservation. Those parts I freely embrace and those parts I would deny. I must take in, and freely accept, all my power, gifts, and talents as my due, seeing clearly my true self as a complete and independent being capable of sharing trust, intimacy, passion and love with others.

Third need. I need to find a partner who is right for me. One who is worthy of all the gifts I have to offer. A partner, with whom I can share a bond of complete trust, so we may build a relationship of intimacy, caring and love. A partner, strong and independent, who is willing to join with me in *my* strength and independence. A partner who will share my life, my love and my aspirations.

Fourth need. I need to be in a healthy relationship of independent equals, each supporting and caring for the other, knowing that every act of kindness will be returned in full measure when needed. Neither partner trying to dominate, or control the other. When I let go my need to be in charge, I gained a better sense of humor about myself.

Fifth need. I need to create things of beauty that have never been seen before. I must express my true nature to create, or die.

Sixth need. I need to share love with my creations.

When I accepted these love based needs, my love poetry started to flow. I tried to imagine the shape, and feel, and qualities of these elements of love. With my words, I created a sacred pool in my landscape where I could drink hope, draw inspiration, find solace, and refresh my joy. Some of my poems sprang from my longing for love, some sprang from having that longing satisfied by my lover. All of them brought me closer to my happiness.

Desire to be Desired

I decided to list the qualities of the woman I would find and share love with, then I wrote a poem to her. This vision made real, would manifest my desire to be desired. I had never experienced the feeling of being desired, and I had a fierce need to realize that in my life. I invoked these feelings by imagining how it would feel to share desire. I sent out this call to the universe. This was my challenge to the one I was seeking. After a time spent living in the open state of pure longing, She answered my ferocity in kind.

Desire to be Desired

I know you not
but still I search
for you who would desire me

Make no mistake
I know of love
I know of care, but not desire

Loved I am, for my goodness
for my kindness
This I know

Desire is still a stranger to my life
In my youth, in all my days
at this age I know it not

so still I search for you

To hear my name fall from your lips
wrapped in passion, husked with want
to hear you call for me

all but breathless for my touch

To see your eyes grow wide as you look in mine
to see your breath catch in your throat
to see your lips grow ripe and moist

eager for my kiss

To taste their sweetness, feel them harden
fierce with need for me
To taste the hollow of your throat

to drink in the nectar of your essence

To feel you drawing up the welling passion from my soul
and feel it spill into the whirling storm that wraps us both
This is my desire

This is why I seek you

Are you out there? Come to me
Join with me in love's sweet passion
Embrace with me, all this night

Desire me

SOUL OF THE GRAPE

I knew the qualities I wanted in the woman I was searching for, but I decided to leave her outward appearance to chance. Now I wanted to woo her. I have always loved the Carpe Diem poetry of Andrew Marvel and Robert Herrick. This 'seize the day' poetry is written to convince a reluctant partner to make love now, because tomorrow may never come. I had Andrew Marvel's poem, *To His Coy Mistress,* in mind when I wrote *Soul of the Grape.*

The qualities I was seeking, for the woman of my dreams, were more likely to be found in someone near my own age. I have known young women, but I much prefer a woman refined by the lessons of maturity. I was struck by the vast difference between grape juice and wine and used that comparison to craft my poem of seduction.

Soul of the Grape is my invitation to a glorious, intoxicating woman, to come to me and share the depths of my passion and love. It is my pledge to her that I will celebrate and value her treasures with my entire being, and I will give of myself to her in full measure. We will celebrate each other's joy and delight, "But," I hear Andrew Marvel clearly singing, "at my back I always hear Time's winged chariot hurrying near". Now is always the time for love.

Poems have the power to enchant, and desires can become manifest. The magnificent woman who now shares my life, was drawn to me by this poem. When we share the soul of the grape, we force the sun to blush.

Soul of the Grape

Grapes ripen on the vine
sparkling in the glowing radiance of the sun
Saving each gilded kiss as sweetness

swelling to delight the eye

Perfect fruit
full to bursting with golden juice
flowing with abundance

Each globe the captive essence of summer's bliss

That same juice
nurtured with care
in time's warm embrace

grows in complexity, subtleness and wisdom

Developing magic
the power to delight the senses
intoxicate the mind

to enthrall my heart with the promise of unimagined passion

How glad I am to not have plucked
that glistening fruit as a callow youth
Behold you now!

What glorious elixir you have become

You are the wine
the transcendent soul
of that perfect golden grape

I long to taste your wine

To savor you with relish and delight
to grow giddy with your scent
to sip as a greedy bird
the nectar of an opulent blossom
drinking deep the essence of your love

To feel you fill me, as I fill you

But wine at last can fade
as all things do beneath the watchful sun
so let us draw forth that cork this day

release it from its glassy sheath

Drink to the fill, both of us each other's passion
surrendering all to the intoxication of love and life
Let us flow together now as one

fill all those empty, inner places with memory and magic

We will make the heavens reel
and force the sun to blush at the brilliance of our love
Come to me. Drink deep our wine

Share with me now the Soul of the Grape

~

I Carry Your Scent

The woman I love lives a distance from me, so we spend time apart in solitary contemplation of our times together. On one long, lonely, drive away from her I was delighted to smell her perfume on me.

The farther I drove from her the more I could feel the tension between us build in intensity.

I knew that, as the days I spent apart from her grew in number so too would my need for her grow. The golden hills of California swept past my car, and these words came to me.

I stopped, wrote them down, and sent them to her. I drove onward.

I Carry Your Scent

I carry your scent where 'ere I go
Sweet memory and perfume wrap me
cloud me as I walk

Your lips on mine
soft and melting,—yield comfort
I dwell, content for now

until need builds anew

~

Touched in the Night

I feel the need to be with my love most sharply in the dark early hours of the morning, when we are apart. I found I could cast out my will and draw the memories of her touch close to me. The connection we share blooms, and sometimes I can actually feel her draw close to me for a few sweet moments, but they are never enough.

Touched in the Night

I awake in the dark with you in my mind
your soft touch lingers, teasing my lips
the scent of you perfumes the air

A feathery breeze caresses me
trails slowly across shuddering skin
thrilling me to my core

I reach forth to draw you in
my arms wrap around the impression of you
formed in the contours of my soul

We embrace, naked before each other
skin pressed to skin, our hearts entwine
we move in passion until the night cries

Our love's splendor burns away the dark
leaving us spent in the glow of the dawn
sharing our breath, together as one

Then slowly, lovingly, you slip away
pause for a moment, as if to stay, then vanish
leaving your warmth within my heart

Your fragrance fresh within my mind

~

You are the Ocean, Wild and Free

I drempt of my lover and the ocean. She asked me the day before if I thought I could handle all her moods. I remembered reading David Deida's, *The Way of the Superior Man*, and he likened the wonderful changeable nature of a woman to the fluid nature of the ocean.

I wrote this poem to reassure her that I wanted her in my life, in all her forms, with all her emotions. I desired nothing less.

I would always be the steadfast rock she could crash against, or flow against, according to whichever emotion she wanted to test me with at the moment. I pledged to love her, and love the testing.

You are the Ocean, Wild and Free

Release the fear that holds you back
Trust the force that flows within
Surrender. Open up your heart
When fear is gone, love remains

I am the shore surrounding you
Calming you in love's embrace
I am the lighthouse on the cliff
Shining love to break the night

I love you in your storm and rage
Your changing nature thrills me
I savor every ebb and flow
Crash your waves against my rocks

Test my strength, my love endures

~

Love in the Deep

I had a dream of ancient leviathans, drifting through glowing oceans, playfully making love. I woke and recorded the dream in the form of a poem. I found that it was easy to write when still in that half awake, twilight state.

The more I wrote, the more the memory of the dream emerged from my own depths. I love the combination of fun and passion mixed with massive, yet delicate, grace.

Love in the Deep

Full moon shines lonely on powerful forms
Reflecting wetly a starless night

Solitary creatures on an endless sea
We find each other

From the kelp matted surface to the inky depths of the sea
We plumb the passions of the leviathans of the deep
Forbidden lust from forgotten times

Brushing aside the thickly matted seaweed
that trails along our contours
Cleaving the waters with our massive tails in a foamy rush

Sporting in our love play

We chase rays of moonlight
In a vault of phosphorescent blue
Trailing glittering bubbles of silver

We dive giddy to the flickering depths
Cold fire liming the outlines of our flanks
Defiant of crushing pressures and numbing cold

We dance in the deep to crying whale songs of love
Whirling to the thrumming organ of a turning earth
Drawn to the pulsing heartbeat beneath us

Crashing together in our need
We push boulders, opening cracks in the ocean floor
Lying thinly over a molten core

Fiery lava jets into chill waters
Pillows upwards, birthing mountains
New land to part the ancient seas

Singing our joy
we drift away spent
Pleased with the mischief of our love

~

CENTERED IN MY BED

After my divorce, I was having problems sleeping alone in my bed. I was still on 'my side of the bed' and feeling strange about it. I talked to a friend and she suggested I sleep in the center of the bed. When I did, I felt a wonderful sensation of power come over me as I stretched my arms and legs out as far as I could. I felt a little like a kid.

Later, I awoke and these lines came out of a dream. They were almost in the haiku form, so I nudged them a bit and this poem was born. I really like the way it captures my sense of independence overlaid with sensual yearning for a partner. I heard the first beat of the shared heartbeat I desired in the final two words of the haiku, so I named my publishing company One Beat Press.

centered in my bed

centered in my bed
naked to night's kiss—I dream
two hearts beat—one song

CHAPTER ELEVEN

THE GIFTS OF GRIEF

11

what's a stab of pain
in a world so filled with joy?
every rose has thorns

I WAS RECENTLY ASKED A QUESTION that floored me. Given that I have transformed my life, and become a fundamentally better and happier man—am I happy that I lost my son?

I will always miss Aaron and would do anything to get him back, but I now know I am powerless to change my loss. What I *can* do is honor the life we shared by making my changed life the best one I can imagine, and feel gratitude for my understanding and acceptance.

Aaron worked daily with troubled children in his educational therapy practice and was a very insightful guy. I believe he saw how my ties to the past held me back. He knew my self-imposed limits kept me from realizing my true potential. I know he worried about me.

It must have been frustrating to him that he could help so many young people, but I remained stubbornly out of his reach. He worked with his students to find, and remove, their blocks to learning which were often caused by faulty images of themselves. Aaron would talk to me about codependency and recommend books to read. He urged me to seek understanding of myself in therapy and to take better care of myself. Alas, I was too mired in complacency to listen. It is irony's cruel joke that his ultimate silence opened my ears to his teaching. I now hear him clearly, and I continue to learn. I see now he was my steadfast companion on this journey. Aaron's greatest lesson to me is that we are the potential of the universe made real.

I finally accept the chaotic nature of the universe, Creation's testing ground. I am learning to tame it with my will. I discovered how to break my self-imposed limits, see what I could be, and make it so. Everything I wanted and needed was within my grasp. I reached out and formed my life anew from the clay of creation.

The gifts I found while grieving were powerful gifts of understanding, and wisdom, that I forged in the fierce furnace of sorrow. I now know I have the power, the right, and the obligation to my true self, to transform my life and make it better. My journey through pain and sorrow led me to see the sweetness of life. I realized I always had everything within me to be happy and feel joy. I just needed to accept who I really was and rejoice in my being. I gained a new perspective of the relationships I share with others. I achieved an acceptance of loss that still brings me peace. I used all that I learned to form a strong vision of my true self.

When I took time to examine my loss, and worked to understand the pain of that loss, I nurtured a deepened love, empathy, and compassion for others—and for myself. There is an old saying, "To light a candle is to cast a shadow." Light divides the dark only for its time, and the polarity of light and dark is needed to perceive anything clearly. Embedded in every act of creation is the ending that heightens its beauty—fragile blossoms floating briefly on the wind.

I learned to savor completely every moment I share with those I love, embracing the knowledge that each unique moment will die so the next may be born. I accept that death will come to everyone I love, and I can live with my losses. To love is to know loss. What matters are the moments of life we share, not the final moment of loss.

My most valued gift is the elixir I found hidden in grief. Love is the greatest power in existence. Love elevates, restores and heals us. We were born from love. We can, and must, love all that we are. We can choose to open our hearts and live our lives surrounded by love. The power of love can triumph even over death. My connections with my lost ones live on in my renewed life. *They* live, tenderly held in my memory of the moments we shared. Every day I gain strength and solace from love invoked.

Now for closure. The real closure I experienced was the closure of grief that came when I reengaged with life and wrote to share these gifts with you. You, in turn, gave me the greatest gift I could ask for, your time to read these words. For all these gifts I am most grateful.

Afterword

Thoughts on Grief and Poetry

where is my lost one?
grieving hearts hurt to hold you
in memory safe

Grief is our way of recovering from loss; the way we experience grief is unique to each of us. The circumstances of our loss are less important than the loss itself, but they do shape our grieving process. Everyone's grieving will differ in its emotional path, duration and intensity, according to the unique circumstances of the loss.

I hope you never experience the loss of a child, but you will lose people you love. Some losses will be expected, and grief may fall lightly on you. Some losses will be a shock, and grief will come to you like a freight train. A death that closes a long full life, usually results in an uncomplicated grief. A sudden death of a young person in their prime often results in a difficult, and complicated grief.

When my mother died at 83, I only shed a few tears at her funeral. I actually felt more relief than sorrow and thought there was something wrong with me. I was concerned that I could not shed enough tears. My fears were unfounded. There was nothing simple about my next grief. I thought I would never stop crying.

Before it could sink in that I was finally an orphan, my son was murdered. The last time I saw Aaron alive was at my mother's funeral, both of us dressed alike in black, surrounded by the sweet stink of lilies from her casket. We had a good long talk, agreed to never argue again, and we sealed our promise with a hug. Not a bad way to say goodbye. Dark joy from dark knowledge.

No one can tell you how to grieve. No one has to. Grief is as natural and fundamental to our existence as breathing. We will all lose someone important to us at some time in our lives, and we may be called on to console a fellow griever.

Grief helps us find balance during our darkest times, and our resilience helps us cope with the worst of those times. Humor in grief is something we find shocking but is so important to our healing. I saw Leonard Cohen in concert after his manager stole his savings. He won a multimillion dollar judgment but could not collect the money, so he went back on the road to support himself.

I saw this 70 year old man on his knees, singing to a packed crowd, while young women in the audience screamed in joy to the words of his poem, *I'm Your Man*. He got up and told the crowd he had lost everything. He went through a period of mourning and anti-depressant drugs, but no matter what he did, "Happiness kept breaking through." Resilience made manifest.

The Emotional States or 'Stages' of Grief

Experts have examined how we behave in response to grief, and have defined the behavioral states we experience as stages of the grieving process. Dr. Elisabeth Kübler-Ross studied the emotional states people experience when faced with their own death. These were the states they went through to accept the greatest personal loss any of us will ever experience, the loss of our own life and future. Later she extended these studies to all types of grief. She defined five stages of grief for us in her seminal book, *On Death and Dying*. These stages are: denial, anger, bargaining, depression and acceptance.

When she faced the grief of her own approaching death, she wrote her last book, *On Grief and Grieving*. I was struck by the grace and warm compassion she showed when she described the emotional states, or stages, of grief. She said these stages are, "part of the framework that makes up our learning to live with the one we lost."

In *On Grief and Grieving*, Elisabeth tried to clear up some misunderstandings people had about the stages. She emphasized that the stages are not rigid and neatly packaged experiences that last for weeks, or months, with formal gates we must pass through before we move forward into the next stage. Elisabeth explained that we may not even go through all of these stages or follow them in a predetermined order. We can sometimes jump back and forth between the stages, in just minutes, as we experience new feelings or gain new insights. The stages of our grief all lead us to greater degrees of acceptance.

Grieving is not a clean, or neat, sort of a process, and the path through these aspects of grief is different for everyone who experiences it. We are all individuals, and we come to our acceptance in different ways. For many of us, grief can be an easy process. This is especially true if we have time to prepare for the loss. When the death of a loved one is a shock, grief can be a deep and overwhelming experience. For a few of us, it can be completely debilitating. Fortunately, most of us are more resilient and can continue to meet many of our daily obligations while still bereaved.

Elisabeth's refinement of the grieving process was very helpful to me, because I found myself often shifting from one aspect of grief to another. The emotional states I experienced were more like emotional cords instead of single notes. There were even times when I felt joy. When I had time to reflect, I was often concerned that I wasn't doing grief right. How could I feel joy for anything when my son was dead? What was wrong with me? I finally gave up trying to follow any kind of programmed path and let my emotions, and growing understanding, take me wherever I needed to go.

I used the five stages of grief to group my poems. The stages often overlapped, and shifted, while I was experiencing them, so my poems may illustrate more than one stage at a time. I drew from Elisabeth's books to discuss the different stages of the grieving process and how they changed me.

At the end of her discussion on Acceptance, Elisabeth identified a final response to grief as the act of reaching out to others as part our re-engagement with life. This act is born from a need to transcend our own grief and help others carry their burden. It is the active choice of compassionate sharing.

Poetry as Therapy

My poems capture views of my inner landscape and fragments of my internal communication between the different levels of my consciousness. The writing process helps me deal with some of the inevitable obstacles that life puts in my way. It also helps me identify, and correct, problems caused by faulty early programming that put limits on my healthy growth and actions.

I see writing as a very focused kind of self therapy. It feels like a beam of laser light created and wielded by me. I turn that coherent light on the dark and hidden parts of my internal landscape to examine what is hidden there. I capture what I find and make it concrete by putting it into words. The process of writing and sharing these poems helped to heal me in three powerful ways.

First, I could capture the overwhelming, but formless, bright blossoms of pain that grief grew within me and make them concrete. The act of putting emotions into words established bounds on my feelings and sharpened my focus, so I could clearly examine how I responded to grief and how the episodes of grief were changing me. This gave me a new perspective on the process that helped me better understand my reactions to the insights I gained while grieving and what those reactions revealed about me.

Words bound things and give us some control over them. Perhaps that's why we have legends about the importance of secret names for people and things. According to the legends, knowing someone's secret name gives you power over them.

If the poem revealed a grief blossom that was 'pulling my strings', at least I could see the connections clearly and then cut the strings if need be. Some of these feelings I chose to keep, like the feelings of empathy that sprang from embracing and understanding my pain. Those feelings are some of the elements of myself that form who I am and who I want to be. Others, like feelings of self doubt, needed to be tempered so they were not self destructive.

Still others, like feelings of self hatred, that stemmed from long term shame and guilt, needed to be weeded out and burned. They served no purpose. I learned that shame and guilt have no long term usefulness. They are only momentary reminders that prick us when we act in a way that is inconsistent with our beliefs and values. This process of examination and self transformation can help us emerge from the grieving process, not only whole but better. Acceptance of loss can bring us the gifts of true self understanding and health.

Second, a burden shared is one lightened. When I share these feelings and memories with you, and others, the power they hold over me is lessened. That sharing lets me drink in a measure of your compassion, and strength, to help me continue to fight my internal battles. We all face these battles, and we are all connected.

By reading this book, you joined this community of fellow travelers and share in this pool of understanding and caring. I take comfort in my belief that when we share these gifts of strength with each other, rather than diminishing that source of strength, we increase it. Perhaps our inner qualities of empathy and compassionate caring are like muscles that grow through use.

Finally, I share these 'pieces of my mind' in the belief they touch something universal within us. In spite of external differences, we are not so different inside. My inner landscapes is unique and malleable, but the features would be familiar to you.

We all have our peaks and valleys, rivers and oceans, parched deserts and hidden glades of wonder. I send you my poems to help you with your own inner struggles and show you how to exercise your empathy muscle.

My poems may throw a light on a hidden inner demon or help to cut a unseen string. I learn something new each time I write a poem and each time one of you shares your interpretation of them with me. By reading this book, you are joining with us to celebrate our connected lives. Remember that we create reality anew with every blink of our eyes. Every moment we share is a new chance to improve the way we view, and interact with, our shared reality.

How I Write a Poem

I wrote many of my poems while I was still grieving heavily and the pain was undiluted. This early time of grieving was a period of denial, intense introspection, disillusionment, and pure abandon from any self censorship. It was an odd sort of freedom from my normal constraints.

For a while, I was writing a poem a day. I would sit in front of my computer, and the words would flow out. It was the only thing I could do at the time, but I now see this writing as some of my best work. At times, I struggle to achieve that same state of abandon only to find it elusive.

At first, writing poetry was an almost unconscious form of art. I was acting from a deep compulsion to expel strange and swirling emotions from my chest and encase them in words. I could not, not write these things

Writing poems let me find a place of peace and solace In the midst of grief. I did not try to filter them but let them describe my inner turmoil as accurately as I could. They were driven by emotion and built of feelings I needed to get outside of me because they could not be contained any longer.

For a while, I would not call them poems because they didn't rhyme. I saw that they contained word patterns that were almost like percussion, much as African based music depends more on rhythm than rhyme. I was later surprised to see that they were much like my Aaron's poetry.

My writing process is a bit different now. I start by thinking about some idea that bubbles up from my subconscious. I get snatches of word combinations that I scribble on scraps of paper and shove into my pocket. I get kind of itchy inside for a while and word patterns start to gel. The actual writing is a free flow of words into my computer over a short period of time. It usually takes thirty minutes or so to construct a poem.

I don't really know where the words are going when I write. The patterns seem to just take form. It's like I have written pieces of the poem already and I am just releasing them. I see the poem as a distillation of thought that transfers my emotions to the outside world.

It feels almost like catching a fish. Each poem has its own wriggling life and moves where it wants to go. If I try to force it in a different direction, the words stop flowing. Then the poem asserts itself and makes me go where it needs to go.

I often switch lines around and find alternate ways of expressing repeating words. This is a sort of game I play with myself. The scribe part of me gets lazy, and then the artist part makes me search for the correct word to capture a necessary nuance.

Sometimes, I get two poems tangled together and I have to put them away until I can straighten them out. I also have snatches of ideas in my slush pile that are premature and waiting for the rest of the poem to catch up. I don't look at these problem children very often, but I know they are there waiting to be born. They will coalesce when the time is right to write.

Poetry to Soften Suffering and Pain

I find my pain is lessened when I share it. I want you to know there is nothing to fear in this kind of pain, it can, and must, be endured. My poems guide you safely through the pitfalls of the grief process and reveal landmarks that will lead you surely forward on your journey to acceptance, and beyond.

Writing poetry helps me with my own understanding and keeps me on track. I deal with sorrow by creating something new, filling some of my emptiness with objects that will endure. As I must endure.

I understand the story of Job now, as a person, not just a dusty lesson from the past. We sometimes need to have our souls thoroughly thrashed, to break us out of our smug, self imposed shells of complacency. To end our casual dismissal of the divine nature of the universe, and embrace the divine within.

Sorry, I'm doing it again. Poetry keeps creeping into every aspect of my life. I see it everywhere now. An appreciation of the dance of electrons, racing through traces and silicon junctions just beyond the glowing phosphors of this screen.

It's kinda hard to turn it off.

Recording the Experiences and Emotions of Grief

Writing helped me gain a measure of control over the grief process and constrained the scope of my powerful emotions. I urge you to try to capture your grief experiences in some fashion. Any personal recording of your feelings, emotional states, and discoveries during this time of your life will be important to you. This record can be in the form of a diary, drawings, voice recordings, or simply discussions with a therapist, or trusted friend.

Any way of capturing your thoughts and discoveries will be helpful in your eventual understanding, and acceptance, of your loss and how that loss changed you.

What's Next — Hacking Grief

I'm writing an expanded version of this book in a new work called *Hacking Grief*, a 'how-to' book with a deeper examination of the grief and transformation processes. I will reveal tools and techniques that will help you transcend grief and restore your faith and trust in life. I plan to continue my research and I write a book about the grieving and transformation processes surrounding the dissolution of relationships, specifically divorce.

You can find more information on my website (www.HackingGrief.com). I will start a blog there, and use the poems contained in *A Landscape of the Soul* as a starting point for you to capture your own grief and recovery experiences and revelations.

I will make the core poems available for download so you can modify them, or use them for inspiration to create your own work. I ask that you share them with the community. You will be able to participate with a username to preserve your anonymity. I want to create a safe forum to discuss grief, ask questions and create interactive poetry. It will be a great exercise in creative compassion, so we can all share the fruits of group healing, growth and discovery.

You don't have to be a poet to capture your feelings. Just open yourself to your emotions and record what you feel. Start with one of my poems and add your own feelings to it.

I invite you to interact with my poems. Replace my words with yours. Play with the words and phrases until you have captured the essence of your feeling.

Abandon yourself to the experience. Don't judge what you write or censor it in any way. This is how you tap into the most creative part of your brain. Release all constraints, find your true voice, and use it to record your experiences. Own this true expression of your innermost self.

Let your writing rest for a while. Walk around and stretch and then reread it out loud. When I did this, I found my emotions were much easier to understand and accept. They were so much clearer to me. If I had to cry about them, I just let the tears flow. The hot, oily tears of grief release some of the accumulated poisons of stress, and are another powerful method of healing.

Sit in a quiet place and relax, breathe deeply. Imagine that you are opening yourself to the moment and think about what you wrote. Write whatever comes to you.

This is how I gained my deepest understanding, and found my most meaningful revelations. These quiet moments of healing were vital to my progress.

Finally, release your work to the group as an act of shared compassion. Release your pain to us so we can help you carry it. Your experiences with grief, your discoveries, and your revelations will help us with our own recovery. Through these exercises, you become your own guide through the changing landscape of your soul.

Please keep an eye on my website. Write with us and heal.

About the Author

Grant Elgin Keller is an engineer, scientist, researcher, graphic artist, writer and poet. Grant has a widely varied scientific background, having worked on the research and development of self healing space systems, low cost rocket engines, and surveillance systems.

Grant has been a ditch digger, a construction worker, a Gasman, an underwater janitor in a shark tank, and he loaded 500 pound bombs by hand on the flight deck of an aircraft carrier during the Vietnam war.

Grant's most enduring work has been to research, understand and explain complex systems.

When confronted with grief, Grant turned to poetry as a way to cope with his feelings and record them. He used his research and visualization skills to examine his emotions and responses to understand what they meant, and how they were changing him. Grant used grief to transform his life and discover happiness. He wants to share his observations with you as part of his final stage of grieving, so he can help you better understand the grief process when you confront it in your life.

Grant's new goal is to create books combining his writing with digital video and art. Please visit his website at www.HackingGrief.com for more information. You can send a message to Grant at: GrantKeller@HackingGrief.com

Grant grew up on Venice Beach, and currently lives in Los Angeles with his pet bonsai tree named Basil. Basil is a bit repressed and has illusions of grandeur.

www.ingramcontent.com/pod-product-compliance
Lightning Source LLC
LaVergne TN
LVHW090953080826
845145LV00003B/990

* 9 7 8 0 9 8 3 9 8 8 3 1 1 *